THE PEACEMAKER

THE PEACEMAKER

*Nixon: The Man, President,
and My Friend*

BEN STEIN

Humanix Books

www.humanixbooks.com

For Aram Bakshian Jr., 1944–2022

Blessed are the peacemakers, for they will be called children of God.

—Matthew 5:9, NIV

CONTENTS

FOREWORD

BEN STEIN AND RICHARD NIXON:
HISTORY'S ODDEST COUPLE

Besides being one of my oldest and dearest pals, Ben Stein is probably the most improbable of all my friends. Even in its currently decadent state, Ben loves the glitz and glitter of the West Coast. I'm allergic to it. Ben's taste in art, music, and decor is unabashedly trendy-modern. My own taste is firmly anchored in the eighteenth and nineteenth centuries. While Ben and I were born the same year—1944—I often felt that my own world view was closer to his parents', Herb and Mildred (who were also cherished friends), than to Ben's.

Ben is also a model of well-directed ambition, of hard work aimed at achieving success in movies, on TV, in fiction and nonfiction publishing alike. I just enjoy writing about subjects I love—humor, history, gastronomy, and the arts—for audiences capable of appreciating them.

And yet for more than half a century, Ben and I have laughed at the same jokes; shared the same hopes, fears, and deep love for our native land; and been inseparable friends. Different as our lives have been, Ben has been an important part of mine, and I believe I have been an important part of his. Perhaps the single strongest unifying theme of our friendship has been a shared affection and respect for a man we both were honored to serve while we were still young: Richard Nixon.

Ben calls him the "peacemaker," a title well earned and one that history is slowly but surely confirming. Richard Nixon laid the early groundwork for a peaceful victory over Communism and the end of the Cold War. Ronald Reagan carried on the great work, brought down the Berlin Wall, and lived to see the evil empire shrivel and die. But the process began under Richard Nixon.

This book is a moving, deeply personal chronicle of the friendship that grew between Ben, the sorcerer's apprentice, and Richard Nixon, first as a brilliant statesman at the pinnacle of power and then as a brooding sorcerer-in-exile, still surveying the world with a masterful gaze. It is also a treasure trove of Nixon quotes, quips, and candid insights, all painstakingly assembled and shared by Ben over the course of years of intimate conversations.

It's no exaggeration to say that what James Boswell was to Dr. Samuel Johnson, Ben Stein was to Richard Nixon: a confidant whose eyes and ears have captured a great man, close up, unvarnished, and endlessly alive in a way no other writer has. There is more of the real Richard Nixon in the pages of this modest memoir than in all the scholarly tomes—and shoddy, mainstream journalism—that fill the shelves of most university libraries.

For all their differences, Ben Stein and Richard Nixon emerge from these pages as kindred spirits: men to whom success did not come easily but through faith, determination, and the guts to try, try, and try again, no matter how bruising the ordeal.

In the end, both succeeded. And this book offers a key to appreciating the incredible nature of that success: a monument to friendship, endurance, and ultimate vindication.

Aram Bakshian Jr.
Washington, DC

PROLOGUE

Up until the resignation of President Richard M. Nixon, Ben Stein, Aram Bakshian, and I shared a suite of offices in the Old Executive Office Building (EOB) as members of the president's personal writing staff. We became fast friends and remain so today.

Aram, a brilliant writer with wide-ranging interests and deep Washington experience, would go on to serve as Ronald Reagan's director of speech writing and continued to publish articles and reviews in numerous publications until his death in 2022. I had come to the Nixon staff from the *National Review* by way of the Office of the Vice President, where I served as Vice President Spiro T. Agnew's chief speechwriter until his resignation. After a tour with President Gerald Ford and some freelance work, I went to work as chief writer for the CEO of Amoco, now BP.

Ben, the third member of our triumvirate, came to the Nixon writing operation from Yale Law School (YLS) after a few dreary stops in the federal bureaucracy. There were some initial doubts about Ben's qualifications, chiefly because he came as the son of the president's chief economic adviser, the brilliant economist Herbert Stein.

But those doubts were quickly dispelled as Ben threw himself into his work. He was totally dedicated to the president, whom they called the peacemaker and for whom he produced, among numerous assigned pieces of presidential prose, the draft of a national energy plan, something that hasn't been done since, and the draft of a coherent health care plan, which, had it been enacted, would have significantly altered the terms of the national debate.

In all, Ben, who because of his unwavering loyalty had become a special favorite of the Nixon family, played an indispensable role in articulating the goals and aspirations of the Nixon administration—an administration of solid accomplishments led by an extraordinary president. The accomplishments were historic—an honorable end to the war in Vietnam; the opening to China, which altered the international balance of power; and a strong and principled defense of Israel, which set the pattern for succeeding administrations. And though he'd lament its takeover by extremists, he can take credit for establishing the Environmental Protection Agency, thus becoming the first—and perhaps the only—green president.

Through Watergate and the years beyond, Ben remained fiercely loyal, defending President Nixon in the media and visiting him frequently for extended conversations on statecraft and politics, uniquely qualifying him to write the book on the real Richard Nixon.

Ben would go on to become a regular contributor on business, politics, government, finance, and the arts for a variety of publications, among them *Barron's*, the *Wall Street Journal*, the

New York Times, Fortune, and the *American Spectator,* would make regular appearances on network news and discussion programs; and would host his own TV show, *Win Ben Stein's Money.* His early days in Hollywood were chronicled in his contemporary classic, *Dreemz.* He is also widely remembered as the droning economics professor in the classic film *Ferris Bueller's Day Off.*

Ben is also known as the author of a series of books aimed at younger readers, talking about investing in a common-sensical way. As Warren Buffett, the most astute and widely admired investor of our times, said of *The Capitalist Code* (Humanix Books, 2017), one of Ben's books, "My friend, Ben Stein, has written a short book that tells you everything about investing. . . . Follow that advice and you will do better than almost all investors."

Writer, economist, pundit, entertainer, friend—Ben Stein is a man of many parts, all of them admirable. But perhaps most admirable is his undying loyalty to one of the most unjustly maligned presidents in American history—a president of great accomplishments who was betrayed, sold out, and railroaded into resigning his presidency.

Ben Stein's deeply felt and evocative *Peacemaker,* written with passion and conviction, represents a significant step in redeeming the reputation of one of our great presidents, Richard M. Nixon.

John R. Coyne Jr.

INTRODUCTION

BLESSED ARE THE PEACEMAKERS

Only if you have been in the deepest valley can you ever know how magnificent it is to be on the highest mountain.

—President Nixon's final remarks at the White House, August 9, 1974

"Blessed are the peacemakers, for they will be called children of God."

This phrase from the book of Matthew keeps running through my mind. I am sitting at the funeral of Richard Milhous Nixon, thirty-seventh president of the United States, at the Richard Nixon Library and Museum, in his birthplace, Yorba Linda, California, about forty miles from Los Angeles. It's a cool, cloudy, drizzling day. Very uncharacteristic of our beloved Southland.

My wife and I are sitting two rows directly behind Julie and David Eisenhower and a few seats away from my parents, Herbert and Mildred Stein.

I recognize dozens of men and women in the immense group of mourners. Some are from the news on TV and in newspapers. Some are family friends. Some are people I worked for and with in the Nixon White House, where I was a speechwriter in 1973 and 1974. Many are from the White House

Mess, where I frequently ate lunch and sometimes dinner with my father. He was a member and then chairman of the Council of Economic Advisers, which entitled him to admission to first the White House Mess and then some higher level of the White House Mess. Only cabinet-level persons could eat in that mess. I, as a speechwriter, was allowed in what was called the Executive Mess.

It was a far more modest eatery in the Old Executive Office Building (now called the Dwight D. Eisenhower Executive Office Building). But my father brought me frequently to the top-level mess (I had the best father there has ever been, and my idea of paradise would be to be back at the White House Mess talking with him), and I was eating with him there one day when he mentioned to me that Elvis Presley was sitting a foot behind me. That was December 20, 1971. (That's another story.)

Back to the funeral. There were several speeches by high pooh-bahs, including Henry Kissinger, Billy Graham, Bob Dole, Governor Pete Wilson—all much-maligned men who were far finer human beings than history had adjudged them at that time.

I saw Tricia and Ed Cox sitting off to my right. Tricia, like Julie, was sitting up straight, and I could see tears running down her cheek.

As I was settling into the low-mood doldrums, I was startled into alertness by the roaring scream of jet engines. Four air force jet fighters were right overhead, and one had just peeled off to make the always mournful "missing man formation." That is the signal that a highly regarded military officer has died either in combat or in some other way.

I explained this to my wife, who comes from a military family. She smiled grimly and said, "For him, it was always combat."

"How true, how true," I said to her. But as I did, I realized that even so, this combatant was probably the greatest peacemaker the Oval Office had ever seen.

Anything at all about Nixon had always made me cry, and so I cried just a little bit more.

When the ceremony was over, I hugged and kissed my parents. Bill Clinton, then president—and a fine president and also eulogist—had very kindly arranged for three large government jets to fly Nixon loyalists, staff, and friends to the funeral. Hillary had objected, so I heard tell, but Mr. Clinton sent the planes anyway for the Washington mourners. My parents were among them. I hugged Julie Eisenhower. She looked beautiful, as always, but her face told a story of unmixed grief.

One of Nixon's many enemies had long ago written that any man who had daughters like Julie and Tricia could not be all bad.

Several buses were waiting to drive the Washington, DC, guests back to their planes. Before my mother and father got on their bus, my mother handed me a bag of groceries from the Safeway at the Watergate, where they lived. Obviously, I could have bought any or all of them in LA. But I felt very lucky to have a living mother giving me grapes. Almost exactly three years later, we were burying her. She was the most intense fan Richard Nixon had ever had. She would have robbed a bank for him.

I take after my parents in many ways . . .

CHAPTER ONE

AN ORDINARY, SOLID CITIZEN AMERICAN:
MY FIRST "MEETING" WITH NIXON

I cannot remember a time when the name Nixon was not floating about in the atmosphere of our home and especially of our neighborhood. From 1948 to 1953, our little family lived on Caroline Avenue in Silver Spring, Maryland. That neighborhood, of perfectly fine middle-class homes but far from mansions, was largely Jewish. In those days, the "good" neighborhoods in Maryland and the District of Columbia were restricted against Jews, Blacks, Asians, Hispanics—anyone who was not a "real American," as FDR had put it. He had told one of his cabinet members that the United States was made by and for Northern European Protestants. No one else, even Jews trying to escape certain death at Hitler's hell holes, was welcome.

We Jews, some of us incredibly fortunate enough to have been several generations in America, were out in Silver Spring, still a perfectly pleasant place, even a paradise, extremely far from the horror show that was Europe in the Hitler years.

For some reason that I have not ever been able to figure out, many of those Jews just hated Nixon. When they said the name "Nixon," they spat it out like Jews in the Pale when they were anticipating a visit from the czar, always accompanied by the rapine and the murder of the accompanying Cossacks. It was almost as if Nixon had done some secret, awful thing that could not be specified but was suggested just by the mention of his name.

As a small child, I picked up that it had something to do with someone named Hiss, who was apparently a Soviet spy but who also might have been a superhero heartily slandered and persecuted by the "evil" Nixon. I was a precocious reader, especially of the *Washington Post*, and well informed on current events, but I never could figure out at that stage of my life what Hiss had done and what Nixon had done. But it was something mysterious and powerful and almost otherworldly.

I do not recall having any discussions with my parents about the subjects of Nixon or Hiss at that time. I do know that they were affected by the fears of Communists in high positions in government and of Communists generally.

One small detail of that fear was that in those halcyon days before there was "racial profiling," we children, even of very young age, were asked to fill out detailed forms about our families, where they were from, and (of special interest) what our fathers' occupations were. (In those days, few mothers worked. Yes, many of our teachers at our beautiful Parkside Elementary School were women, but, indeed, few of them were married.) By the way, in those far-off days, Montgomery County, Maryland, schools were racially segregated by law. It was a crime for Black people to attempt repeatedly to enroll at a whites-only school. Yes. A crime. The only Black person we ever saw at school was Willie, a Black former U.S. Army soldier who had found work as the school janitor. The school was heated in winter by a coal furnace. Willie had to get up very early on frosty mornings and drive in from his home far out in the forests of upper Montgomery County (which we thought of as being as forested and far away as if they were in Maine, now heavily built up) to get to Parkside.

There, he shoveled coal into the furnace to keep us white boys and girls warm all through the day. Between the shoveling, he walked up and down the hallway at our school tossing out resin and using it to sweep up the floors.

Even then, I was repulsed by the mistreatment of Willie. For him to have been in the army, serving as a truck driver and freight loader in the Red Ball Express, carrying fuel, food, and ammunition for the U.S. forces fighting the Wehrmacht while being shot at by Nazi snipers, to then be working at a school that would not have allowed his children to attend was disgusting to me. He retired when I was a sixth grader. I gathered money and bought him a trophy.

As I said, I had to write down on a form what my father's occupation was. We were then to read the form to our classmates and teachers in a facet of elementary school life called show-and-tell. My mother was so concerned that out of my little mouth would come a word that sounded too much like "Communist" instead of "economist." So she had me say to the class of elementary school kids that my pop was a "statistician" instead of an economist.

It was a mouthful, but I did it.

Meanwhile, back on Caroline Avenue, on our brand-new Magnavox TV, in its immense blond wood cabinet, there were stories about something called HUAC, the House Un-American Activities Committee. This entity was deeply hated in our neighborhood, as far as I could tell. I was not sure why.

I had no clear idea at all what it did, only that it was hated by the same people who hated Nixon. What the connection was, if any, I did not know.

Then there were TV news stories about Richard M. Nixon, who was starting to become truly famous. Again, it had something to do with the mysterious Hiss. But I still did not know who that was. (More about him to come.)

And I started to see images of Mr. Nixon on the TV screen and also on the pages of the *Washington Post* and our afternoon newspapers, the *Daily News* (a tabloid) and the *Washington Star*. The photos in the *Post* often were accompanied by text that noted what a horrible human being Nixon was. There was also a famous political cartoonist at the *Post* named Herbert Block, whose nickname, or nom de plume, was Herblock. He simply loathed Nixon and drew him with a gangster-style slobby beard and sometimes wielding a dripping meat cleaver. (I later got to know Herblock when I worked for a summer as a copyboy for the *Post*. I worked a late-night shift. My little desk was right outside Mr. Block's drafting room. Late at night, he would often show up with his latest artwork for us copyboys to appraise. One of the copyboys was a young Black man. He hated being shouted out for as "boy," which was the practice when a writer or an editor had a document he wanted to be brought somewhere, and protested against the practice, and I joined in. It was my first "civil rights" protest.)

The pictures and the cartoons mystified me. Mr. Richard Nixon did not look like a bad guy. He did not, in fact, have a beard or a five-o'clock shadow. He was not wearing a Nazi uniform. He was not wearing a swastika armband. The images behind him were not in German or Cyrillic. He just looked like an ordinary, solid American citizen. He looked a lot like the few male teachers we had at Parkside. He looked astonishingly like our next-door neighbor on Caroline Avenue.

Why did his name call forth such sneering hatred? It certainly didn't at our house, at least as far as I recall it.

Somewhat earlier had come my first encounter with the real Richard Nixon. I do not recall the exact date or even the approximate date. I just recall that the 1952 presidential election was going on. As everyone knows, the Republican ticket was General Dwight David Eisenhower, supreme Allied commander Europe (SACEUR) in World War II. His veep would be Richard M. Nixon, then a U.S. senator from the Golden State of California.

That, in itself, was cause for further hatred and sneering at Mr. Nixon in our little neighborhood. Why? Who knew? Apparently, according to overheard snippets of conversation from neighbors, amply fortified by angry accusations in the *Washington Post*, especially by Drew Pearson, a columnist whose widely read words appeared on the same pages as the comics in the *Post*, Richard Nixon had done some terrible things to win his election for U.S. senator against a much-beloved woman named Helen Gahagan Douglas.

What these terrible things were was never clear to me. He had apparently called Mrs. Douglas a Communist. But there was never any clear evidence of those comments. And the *Star* ran pieces insisting that Mrs. Douglas's Democratic opponents in the primary had called her far worse—and there was documentation of those words. So, again, lots of smoke but no fires that I could see.

And my parents, both highly educated economists and well informed, did not sneer at Nixon and could not show me where in our newspapers Nixon's (allegedly horrible) comments about Mrs. Douglas appeared.

Senator Nixon's highly publicized efforts against Alger Hiss and his part in something called a "witch hunt" against alleged Communists in government were well known. His work in that arena was necessary and even lifesaving, as far as we in our little family were concerned. They could be cruelly mocked and lambasted in the *Post*. But in our little house, Nixon's efforts seemed to make sense. After all, if there really were subversives in the government, we wanted them out of there, and quick.

From the earliest possible age, I had been inoculated against Communism and any form of "totalitarianism."

My parents had both been strongly anti-Communist and antifascist all their lives, as far as I knew. We were taught at Parkside that life in a Communist country was a slave life. There was fear, violence, no civil rights—nothing but misery. Even as a very young child, I read *Darkness at Noon* by Arthur Koestler, about Stalin's show trials. It was genuinely terrifying. By far the worst nightmare I have ever had was about yours truly, even as a small child, being made to "confess" horrible acts of treason and sabotage against the Soviet Amerika. (Yes, I recall that spelling from my dream.) In my nightmare, I was made to stand against a brick wall along with some other "criminals" and await shooting.

Of course, we were also taught that Nazism was even worse in that we Jews were singled out for torture, starvation, murder, and general immiseration. But as we were taught, Stalinist Communism was not much different from Nazism.

So for Nixon to be hated for being strongly anti-Communist was inexplicable. For Hiss seemingly to be admired and considered a martyr for being an agent for the Communists was utterly incomprehensible. Why would a man whose fame was largely derived from unmasking an agent of a hideous foreign power and a horrifyingly evil ideology be hated for it?

Back to square one: my first "meeting" with Nixon. The 1952 campaign was underway. My hometown, Silver Spring, Maryland, had a small Baltimore & Ohio Railroad station on Georgia Avenue. It was right next to an International Harvester tractor dealership. There was to be a small rally for the GOP ticket on the train tracks of the B&O station. I do not recall if General Eisenhower was to be there, but Senator Richard Nixon was.

My parents took me to the station. At age seven, I stood on my father's shoulders and watched Mr. Nixon speak. He was startlingly close to us. I have no recollection of what he said. I do recall that he swung his fists often to underline whatever point he was making. And I recall that he was a handsome man. Then, we would have said that he was "movie-star handsome." He bore no resemblance at all to Herblock's frighteningly ugly cartoons.

I also recall that after Mr. Nixon's remarks, some of us in the audience came up close to the back platform and asked him questions. I do not even remotely recall what the subjects were. I just remember that he had a warm, engaging smile and that he took my little hand and smiled at me.

Very soon, he was gone, and one of the last of the whistle-stop train rallies was over.

In the campaign, General Eisenhower was a divinity. He was largely beyond reproach or even questioning. All of the endemic anger of the press was directed at Mr. Nixon and none at the SACEUR.

There were many questions in the *Post* about something called a "slush fund." It was a fund supposedly hidden from the law, given by local businessmen in Southern California. It allowed Nixon to buy things he should not have been allowed to buy. That turned out to be a pure invention of the press, a complete phony.

There were many questions about a man whom our neighbors hated as if he were Satan, Joseph R. McCarthy. There was a raft of questions and rage about something called the "China lobby," which I did not understand at all. I still don't. They were against the Red Chinese. What was wrong with that?

What I did see—but did not understand—was a raging subterranean torrent of fury at the handsome man with the friendly smile and the engaging handshake. I have never understood it.

CHAPTER TWO

AMERICA IN THE 1950S: A NONBORING DECADE OF PEACE, PROGRESS, AND PROSPERITY . . . BUT WE WERE SCARED

There are many lies about our beloved America. One of them is that the 1950s were a boring decade. That's not even remotely true. That decade was when America went through many challenges, surmounted many racial and racist barriers, fought a bloody and cruel war in Korea, and emerged at its end a completely different nation.

Just as a fantastically important example, in 1949, the public schools in this country were, in many states and counties, segregated by race. This segregation was not only in the Deep South—say, Louisiana, Mississippi, Alabama, and South Carolina—it was true in Florida; Texas; Kansas (not all of Kansas); Oklahoma; Missouri; Maryland; Delaware; Kentucky; parts of Indiana; the nation's capital, Washington, DC; and also Tennessee.

This segregation by race was legal. If a mother or father chose to challenge the law that imposed segregation, he or she could try to go to court and attempt to get a court order compelling integration. Such an attempt was bound to fail. The courts of this country had repeatedly said that "properly" enacted (i.e., by a legislature) school segregation was allowed by the

Constitution. The British statesman William E. Gladstone had called the Constitution "the most wonderful work ever struck off at a given time by the brain and purpose of man."*

The U.S. Supreme Court had repeatedly said that school segregation by race was permitted by the Constitution if the resulting school system had "separate but equal" facilities. This was laid out especially clearly in the famous Louisiana case that reached the Supreme Court, *Plessy v. Ferguson*.

In many of the movies and radio shows and early TV shows of the era, Black people were portrayed as stupid, lowlifes, criminals, foolish, barely human at all. Of course, there were exceptions. Mammy in *Gone with the Wind* was smart. So was Sam in *Casablanca*.

The armed forces of the nation were still largely segregated by race. Black men could serve as truck drivers or dishwashers or freight loaders. They could—and with extreme success did—occasionally serve as fighter plane pilots. But this great and glorious nation was still largely one big pot of racism enacted into law in many venues.

By the end of the 1950s, there were still segregated school districts in the Deep South. But by and large, and with immense controversy, the nation's schools south of the Mason–Dixon line were either integrated or in the process of being integrated. The military was thoroughly integrated and had been in the Korean War.

But that took a struggle. The state of Virginia went so far in 1958 as to engage in a policy of "massive resistance" against integration. That policy called for literally closing all the public

---

* William E. Gladstone, "Kin Beyond Sea," *North American Review*, September–October 1878, 185.

schools in Virginia rather than see them integrated. Obviously, it did not last long, but it was a measure of how much resistance to desegregation there was. By 1960, the schools in Virginia except for a few in the extreme southwestern corner of the state were integrated.

There were wholesale riots in Little Rock, Arkansas, over desegregating Central High School. The National Guard had to be "federalized" by President Dwight Eisenhower to suppress mob violence and allow a Black little girl to attend that high school. Now Central High School is a historical landmark because of its lengthy on-camera time in the mid-1950s. But by 1959, Central High School was thoroughly racially integrated. Many white children had dropped out of that school, but it was certainly open to Black students.

In really Deep South states like Mississippi, there was still complete school segregation. But otherwise, school segregation, which had seemed as permanent as Mount Rushmore, was largely (not completely) gone by the end of the 1950s. Getting there was anything but dull. There were riots, sit-ins, shocking violence by the police on civilians.

Then there was the amazing phenomenon known as "McCarthyism." An obscure U.S. senator from Wisconsin had broken into the stratosphere of fame by alleging in a speech in 1949 in Wheeling, West Virginia, that there were large numbers of card-carrying Communists at work within the U.S. State Department. The exact number fluctuated over time. But the allegations by McCarthy stirred up the nation in a big way. Just the thought that there were sellouts betraying their country to the Soviets as we were fighting a bloody war against Communism in the Korean Peninsula was deeply unsettling. McCarthy went from obscurity to superstardom more or less overnight. Reds in our own government? What could be worse?

The allegations were cued by the master of all allegations, Senator Joe McCarthy, to wit, that Alger Hiss, a high State Department official, was a Communist and a spy.

As noted above, Richard Nixon played a large role in exposing Hiss. Nixon worked with Whittaker Chambers, an editor at *Time* who claimed that he had been a member of a Communist cell in DC and that Alger Hiss had been a high-ranking fellow member of that cell, to unmask Hiss and other Communists in government.

Hiss, a Boston Brahmin with many pals in the left-wing elites all across the country, had denied everything. But after a great deal of drama, Hiss was found to have been lying under oath to a congressional committee and eventually went to prison for perjury. (Several decades later, when the USSR collapsed, many KGB files were released and decrypted. These "Venona decrypts" showed unequivocally that Hiss had been not only a Communist Party member but an actual spy. Hiss's inside information, passed to the Soviets and then to the North Koreans, was crucial in starting the Korean War, a bloody event that cost about fifty-five thousand American lives and about one million Korean lives. Predictably, Hiss still has many defenders in the mass media and the "prestige" universities of America. Nixon does not have a friend at those once revered spots.)

The early 1950s were a time when there was real nationwide fear that the U.S. government was thoroughly infested with Communists bent on the destruction of our way of life. Nixon's accomplishments in that realm regarding Hiss were a major factor in his being chosen as running mate for Dwight Eisenhower.

Had there been no Hiss, there might well have been no Nixon as a national and international figure of fame and power.

The whole look of America had changed in the supposedly somnolent 1950s. If you were to look at 1949 automobiles, they still resembled 1930s autos, although some changes had been made. By 1959, American cars were sleek beasts with massive tail fins and three hundred horsepower V8 engines.

Movies were overwhelmingly black and white in 1950. By 1959, it was a rare movie indeed that was not in color.

In the decade of the 1950s, the Soviet Union acquired, first, the atom bomb, largely thanks to the Communist spies Julius and Ethel Rosenberg and Ethel's brother, David Greenglass. The Soviets also had developed intercontinental rocketry to a level far beyond what we had in the United States. Then a few years later, they had the hydrogen bomb.

That meant endless fear of a sudden nuclear attack. There were school drills, where we would "duck and cover" under our little desks. Then there were uprisings in Eastern Europe. Riots at a shipyard in Gdańsk. A major uprising in Hungary. Soviet tanks rolling down major streets in Budapest. Unrest in East Germany—obviously a very sensitive place as far as the Soviets were concerned. It looked more and more as if we were in a prewar world rather than a postwar one. Only this time, the war, if it came, would mean the end of the world.

If I dwell on this issue—Communism—it's because America did too. Alongside racial matters and controversies, fear of domestic and Soviet Communism was *the* big issue of the 1950s.

On the plus side in a huge way, medicine improved. We got a polio vaccine that dramatically uplifted the summer season. Children could go swimming at neighborhood pools without their parents having to fear that the kids would come back with a cold that turned into paralysis.

So, yes, the civil rights of Black people had improved dramatically. Yes, we had far better cars. Yes, we had movies in color. Yes, we saw that the Soviet monolith was not invincible.

Yes, there were immense strides in medicine. But we were scared. Scared of violence by and against Blacks. Scared of the Soviets. We were just plain scared.

And what was Richard Nixon doing in this era?

He was vice president to General Dwight David Eisenhower, a beloved president, a stupendous World War II hero with a friendly grin. He was mocked and belittled for his alleged stupidity by leftist snobs. But he had done heroic work in Western Europe. And he seemed like the type of guy who would sit down and play cards with you, and you would have fun. And he was in fact an extremely good poker player. He had won a large portion of the down payment on his postwar life playing poker in the Navy.

Contrary to the "ideas" of the leftists, Nixon played a huge role in the humbling of Senator Joseph McCarthy. Once McCarthy, on the advice of a genius staff member named Roy Cohn, a really brilliant but troubled human being, started to go after the U.S. Army, he was on Ike's bad list. McCarthy was a supercatalyst for some in the GOP but a great embarrassment to the New England aristocrats who were still a big part of the party in the 1950s.

He had to go. Ike and other high pooh-bahs decided he had to go. Nixon was the man who ran the arrangement that entrapped McCarthy and emasculated him.

Although this had been a consummation devoutly wished by the Left, Nixon got absolutely no credit for it. To this day in 2023, Nixon is somehow connected with McCarthy as a smearer of innocent people. Although when pressed, even intelligent persons cannot think of any innocent people that McCarthy ruined. There must have been some, but they are hard to recall. (There is a superb book about McCarthy that is highly complimentary to Mr. Nixon. The book is called *A Conspiracy So Immense* by a fine historian named David Oshinsky.)

Nixon was also said to have been a player behind the Hollywood blacklist perpetrated by the House Un-American Activities Committee (HUAC). The HUAC blacklist supposedly wrecked the Hollywood careers of many innocent people. I don't know who they were. I don't doubt it though. (I've been blacklisted for being a Nixon aide and a conservative in Hollywood. Being blacklisted is not fun at all.)

But of course, except for the briefest of moments, Richard Nixon was not even in the House. He was a senator. He had nothing to do with HUAC, although he certainly was friends with some of its members.

There was, as noted, a good-sized rebellion in Budapest against Communist/USSR domination. At one point in 1956, the powers that be in Hungary opened some border crossing points into neutral Austria. Hundreds of thousands of Hungarians fled their homes to go to Austria and many thence to the United States.

The United States was excited but also nervous about this uprising. We saw it as a sign that the Soviet bloc was not invulnerable. But we were also afraid that the Russians would use it as an excuse to send their massive Red Army into Western Europe. Some U.S. legislators were also concerned that an influx of skilled Hungarian labor would compete with skilled U.S. laborers.

Ike sent Nixon to Austria to cheer up the Austrians. He also wanted Nixon to greet the exodus of Hungarians and tell them they were welcome. Nixon went to several crossing points and—in the bitter cold—held out his hand to welcome whatever Hungarians turned up. When he got back to the United States, he spoke about what a triumph the uprising was for freedom and free speech.

For this, he also got no thanks, except from General Eisenhower, who behaved nobly.

Meanwhile, the president had some worrisome health problems. He had suffered a serious heart attack in 1955 while playing golf at Burning Tree. Nixon had sat in for him at some cabinet meetings and other major events. The Left made innumerable "jokes" about Nixon stepping on Ike's oxygen tube. But there was no evidence at all of Nixon seeking to overstep his bounds.

In 1956, Ike suffered a medium-sized stroke. His doctors put him in Walter Reed Army Medical Center for several weeks, and soon he was his usual energetic, astute self. Again, there were no signs at all that Richard Nixon (I'll refer to him from here on out as RN) had sought to overreach, but he was still the butt of endless ridicule.

At this point, I was in sixth grade at Parkside Elementary School. (It was called Parkside because it was next to a beautiful, enormous park called Sligo Creek Park, named for one in the British Isles.) It had become clear to me that there were certain kids who got teased and bullied on the playground and in the halls no matter what they did. They just gave off an aura of trying too hard, of being excessively vulnerable, of either crying or even looking sad when teased.

They also were "too smart" and made other pupils feel as if they were stupid or lazy.

I thought I was such a person. I thought I saw much of myself in Nixon. At this very long remove from my days in elementary school, I can see that I was not particularly mistreated, certainly not compared with the hell hole of a junior high school, Montgomery Hills, that I was about to attend.

I had checked out a simple biography of RN from the tiny library at Parkside. (Somehow we had managed to learn to read and write and calculate without computers or broadband.) In this biography, Nixon was portrayed as a sad and lonely young man. His brother had died of tuberculosis. His mother had worked as a nurse while the brother lay dying. His father had only modest work. At one point he owned a lemon farm, but (Nixon later lamented) he sold it before they discovered oil on it.

But most of all, Nixon was not considered loveable. At least so this biographer wrote. When he first fell in love with Patricia Ryan, soon to be his wife, Nixon would drive her to her "dates" with other high school boys (or maybe college boys) just so that he could spend time with her. I found that agonizingly touching then and I still do, roughly seventy years later.

In any event, there was something about Nixon I just found spellbindingly touching. In 1956, when Ike and Dick ran for president and vice president against Governor Adlai Stevenson and Estes Kefauver, an outright segregationist from Tennessee who had defeated the also-ran Senator John F. Kennedy for the veep slot, we had a debate in our horrible junior high school civics class.

I took the GOP side and debated ferociously, as I then thought, for Ike and Dick.

Now a slight but important side note. In 1952, my parents hired a well-known architect to design and build a home for my sister, Rachel, my parents, and me in a much nicer neighborhood than the one we had been in.

The land for that neighborhood had been owned by (what we then thought was) the fabulously rich Col. E. Brooke Lee, an original patriarch of Montgomery County and a relative of Robert E. Lee. His son-in-law was a handsome, self-confident Princeton grad and World War II combat hero named David Scull. He was a scion of a famous Philadelphia family whose antecedents had founded Princeton, a real estate man, and also a Republican political figure in Montgomery County.

The Sculls had a son roughly one year older than I was. He was a smart, charming, startlingly handsome fellow named David Lee Scull. I was wildly fond of the Scull family and worked at ingratiating myself with them. One way to do that was to be a feverishly energetic child Republican. And one way of doing that was to be strongly pro-Nixon.

Politics is personal and not professional, as the saying goes.

I thought I saw a good bit of Nixon in David Scull, the father. As I look back upon it now, there is little resemblance. Not only do they not look the same, but they came from wildly different social backgrounds. Long ago, I came upon a book on *Social Register* weddings of the mid- and late 1930s. Sure enough, there were Mr. and Mrs. Scull. I am very sure Richard Nixon is not in any such document.

As the 1950s chugged along, with the advent of rock 'n' roll, probably the first mass entry of Black culture into the mainstream of American culture, the elites of American life continued to hate Nixon. Again, I did not see why. As far as I could tell, obviously as far as the GOP could tell, Nixon was a perfectly capable man.

The Left still held powerful grudges against him for exposing Alger Hiss. Why that would be when Hiss was a spy for a dangerous international enemy, I had no idea. I did not know then that ideology and psychological magnetism trumped almost every other consideration, even patriotism.

What I said in my 1956 debate I cannot recall.

At that time, there had just been a battle in the northern portion of the then French colony of Vietnam. To everyone's surprise, a "clever" French strategy to bring the Communist rebels out into the open where French and U.S. air power could subdue them had turned into a rout of the French by the barefoot soldiers of the Communist rebels.

Some Americans suggested that the United States should use nuclear weapons on the Communist rebels. There were rumors that RN had endorsed such a bizarre role in the middle of some of the densest jungles on earth. But RN in fact powerfully resisted any large-scale use of U.S. arms to protect the French colonial empire.

Instead, he asked for the four-power split-up of the former French colony in Indochina. This, at an early stage of Richard Nixon's career in high executive power, was perhaps the first sign of RN's inclination toward peace when there was any other option.

As noted, Nixon also resisted the Southern Democrats who had resisted the Ike and Dick civil rights initiatives of the mid-1950s. These were the first major attempts to legislate equality in voting, housing, travel, and accommodations. The attempts were only partly successful. But Nixon was always in there pitching for civil rights. His mother's family had always been proequality for the Black man. RN was not about to lose that legacy, even to get the help of a powerhouse like James Oliver Eastland, U.S. senator from Mississippi, or Richard Brevard Russell Jr., U.S. senator from Georgia, in legislative battles.

None of that mattered. The Left and much (not all) of the mass media knew that they hated "Tricky Dick" Nixon. (What his "tricks" were, some seventy years down the road, I still have no clue.)

But I knew I liked Nixon. My father did too, as I recall. I do not recall at all what my mother's inclination was at that point. By the time RN was in the White House though, he had no supporter as passionate as Mildred Stein.

By 1960, Richard Nixon was running hard for president. The Left still hated him. So did some on the *Social Register* Right. The GOP at that point, as now, was divided into class lines. There were the gunslingers like Joseph McCarthy and Pat McCarran and the blue bloods like Henry Cabot Lodge. They had never thought Nixon was "good enough." But then they probably never thought that Ike was good enough either.

That election was my second "encounter" with Richard Nixon. He spoke at a venue in Silver Spring (possibly the boys' gym at Montgomery Blair High School). There was a huge crowd to hear him speak. They were respectful and didn't yell or scream. (A few days later, John F. Kennedy spoke at the boys' gym at Blair. His audience, mostly women and girls, definitely were yelling and screaming, as if we were watching a rock star. As a woman seated near me said, "The man has lights inside him." I heard people say that about JFK many times during his tragically short life.)

My father had met Nixon at some kind of function in the District of Columbia on the future of the economy given by his colleagues at the Committee for Economic Development. CED was a group of very big businessmen and labor leaders and farm bureau men. (The American Farm Bureau Federation was an organization of owners of extremely large farms and ranches. Not your mom-and-pop farmers in coveralls.) I well remember meeting the head of General Motors—as I recall, a man named Harlow Curtice. GM made the Corvette, a super-cool car, and that made me worship Mr. Curtice.

My pop brought me to a small, brief reception with Mr. Nixon after the speech.

RN had spoken, as I thought then and now, intelligently about what the country had accomplished in the Eisenhower/ Nixon years. He led off by talking about the civil rights acts that the GOP had gotten enacted, the first major milestones for Blacks in America since Reconstruction. Even then I thought he was brave for taking on this subject, considering that Maryland was still largely segregated. He then spoke about how we were catching up to and overtaking the USSR in the "space race," as it was called.

Defense was an obsession in our household. JFK had made much of what he called the "missile gap," and it was heartening to hear RN's reassurances.

He then talked briefly about the three Ps of the Eisenhower years: peace, progress, and prosperity. I had no idea whatsoever that someday I would be a White House speechwriter for that self-same Richard Nixon. But I do recall that RN spoke without notes or a prepared speech or a teleprompter. I was impressed. He gave an impression of earnest love of his country.

At the tiny reception after RN's talk, I had the effrontery to tell him that he was a great speaker and that I admired very much the fact that he had spoken without notes. He looked at me kindly and shook my hand. He seemed to know my pop and called him Herb. That made me superhappy. I have always made a fetish of my pride in my father. To think that a man of RN's stature called him by his nickname made me happy.

Somehow, the conversation turned to family pet dogs. RN somehow knew that we had a small dog. He had an extremely famous dog named Checkers, a cocker spaniel. Checkers had been used with great effect in a speech that Mr. Nixon gave in 1952 when he was alleged to have benefited from an unethical "slush fund" set up by Southern California businessmen. The whole thing turned out to be a phony smear. Nixon went on TV and listed all of his family's meager assets and where they came from. He said that the only gift he had gotten from a businessman was a dog named Checkers and that he would never give up that dog because (as he said) "the girls love him." (He was, of course, referring to his wonderful daughters, Tricia and Julie.) That was as far as the conversation went, but, again, he vibrated with kindness and a love of dogs. He was my kind of guy.

RN was running hard against John F. Kennedy, the junior senator from Massachusetts. I knew that JFK was the son of a fabulously rich, influential Democrat named Joseph Kennedy. That man had made his fortune—so one heard—from being a whiskey bootlegger during Prohibition. FDR had appointed him U.S. ambassador to the Court of St. James's. It was an odd choice because Joe Kennedy was explicitly pro-Nazi, and Britain was the bulwark of freedom and anti-Nazi heroism.

Joseph Kennedy was also an explicit anti-Semite. In those days, many prominent white people were. Still, it was a surprising choice for FDR, who was a huge favorite of Jewish voters.

JFK had been a war hero fighting the Japanese in the Solomon Islands in World War II. A Japanese destroyer had cut JFK's patrol torpedo boat in half, and he had saved much of his crew. He was a good-looking guy. A "babe magnet." A well-dressed rich guy with a stylish woman of New York society as his equestrienne bride. The media loved him.

Nixon's father had been a bus driver and a lemon farmer. His mother was a Quaker. His wife had worked hard all her life. He was not stylish.

But he was my kind of guy. The salt of the earth. A patriot. A family man. He had a lovely wife and two simply beautiful daughters, one of whom became a close friend of yours truly.

He also was a brave man. In 1958, RN had gone on a "goodwill" tour of South America. At that time, anti-American, violent ideas had taken hold of a large part of the students, workers, and "intellectuals" of our neighbors to the south. At several stops, Nixon was attacked by mobs of students and agents provocateurs shouting vile anti–United States slogans at him and his wife.

In Caracas, a large, angry group of students organized by violent Communist agitators stoned his car, smashed the car's windows, explicitly threatened to kill him, spat on him, and through it all, he maintained his calm and dignity. His "protection" by the Secret Service and the Venezuelan government was hugely inadequate. He must have been terrified, but he shone through in all his courage, and the strength of his faith in his God, the God of peace, would protect him and Pat.

That was probably his high point as vice president. His poll ratings in the United States were at their highest point ever. In a series of impromptu debates at an American National Exhibition of a typical American kitchen, Nikita Khrushchev, head of the Central Committee of the Communist Party of the Soviet Union, shouted that he did not believe that a typical American kitchen could possibly be so modern and airy. It was in fact a modest kitchen by the standards of the day and especially by modern American standards.

In that debate, Khrushchev told Nixon, "We will bury you." By that he meant that Marxism would prove prophetic and that Soviet-style Communism would surpass the immense advantage that the United States had over the USSR in living standards.

Nixon answered firmly but peacefully that freedom would always triumph over dictatorship. Amazingly, that debate was arranged by Bill Safire, the PR genius who later wrote many great books and who defended RN brilliantly in his column in the *New York Times*. Mr. Safire was a great friend to my parents and to me. His friendship to me was life changing.

Again, Mr. Nixon shot up in the polls after that "kitchen counter" debate with Khrushchev.

Nixon also stood up for the Black man in an unstinting way. As noted, the decade of the 1950s began with America as an uncompromisingly segregated nation. Under Ike, who was considered to be a reluctant integrationist, and Dick, who was considered by the Left and much of the media to be the devil, America began inching toward being an integrated nation.

There were riots and beatings of integrationist Blacks, especially of the so-called freedom riders, who sought to integrate southern Greyhound and Trailways bus services. There were still occasional, rare, but morally horrible murders of Black men who seemed to be too "uppity" to Klansmen and other criminals.

The horrifying murders of two Jewish civil rights workers, Andrew Goodman and Michael Schwerner, near Philadelphia, Mississippi, along with their Black colleague Andrew Chaney in 1964 were sad reminders of how much further we had to go.

In all these conflicts, Nixon stood unwaveringly for the rights of the Black man. In these conflicts, Nixon was often pitted against powerful southern representatives and U.S. senators who were as staunchly for segregation as Nixon was for equal rights and integration.

In particular, he was often opposed by Senate majority leader Lyndon Johnson, Democrat of Texas, who routinely called Black Americans by what we now know as the "N-word."

Yet despite what looks to me like perfect or close-to-perfect behavior as VP to Dwight Eisenhower, RN was still the media's favorite bogeyman. To repeat, for reasons I have never understood, he was called Tricky Dick after he defeated Helen Gahagan Douglas for the U.S. Senate. What he did that was especially tricky has (again) never been clear. Yet there he was, day and night, Tricky Dick. The whole notion of the party of Lyndon Johnson and Robert Byrd (Klan high pooh-bah in West Virginia and then high-ranking U.S. Senate Democrat) calling Richard Nixon Tricky Dick was just a mystery.

Tricky Dick? Compared with LBJ? It's a joke. But a cruel joke.

So why? Why did the "beautiful people" loathe Nixon? Wasn't it just the bullies picking on the vulnerable, shy boy on the playground? Wasn't it just me, writ large?

When the 1960 election came upon us, it was before the Freedom Summer lynchings in Mississippi. Hubert Horatio Humphrey was the leading Democratic presidential candidate at the beginning of the primary season. He was a committed liberal. Just as a fine example of how committed he was, Humphrey bought a home and lived in it in an unrestricted neighborhood in Bethesda, Maryland, very close to my area, Silver Spring. As far as was reported, Senator Humphrey was the *only* senator who did not live in a "restricted"—that is, *judenrein*—neighborhood.

For that reason, my parents gave to his campaign. I had the pleasure—no, the honor—of meeting him at a fund raiser for him at the Sheraton Carlton. He was a beaming, pleasant man indeed.

But he was simply buried in a blizzard of Kennedy family money in West Virginia. That was a key state because it was said that if a Catholic could win in heavily Protestant Christian West Virginia, he could win anywhere. Trustworthy Kennedy family retainers were employed to drop off paper bags full of money to precinct bosses all around the Mountain State.

Something like that happened to Richard Nixon on a national scale. Yes, he had been a fine vice president. Yes, his term was scandal-free. But money talks.

And party loyalty talks. There were debates. Richard Nixon could have looked a lot better if he had better makeup. He could have worn a smile. But he did a creditable job. He ran a creditable campaign.

He was competent. But he did not have lights inside him. And he did not have the Kennedy family money inside him. Most of all, he did not have Mayor Richard Daley of Chicago making sure that Cook County gave JFK just enough votes to make sure he won Illinois despite Nixon's wide margin in the rest of the state. And he did not have Lyndon Johnson and his pals making sure he got enough votes in what was then Democratic, segregationist Texas to make sure JFK won Texas—and thereby hung the election.

Sad, but frankly, at that time in my life, I was too young to vote. And I paid little attention to politics. Yes, I surely liked Nixon a lot. Yes, I surely thought that a Republican government was what the country needed. But what I really wanted in November of 1960 was a fast car and a girl named Gay Patlen to be my girlfriend. I ultimately got the car.

I felt sorry when I saw the emotionally crushed faces of the Nixon family on election night. Mr. and Mrs. Nixon knew politics. They knew every precinct in every state. They knew they had won in Texas and Illinois but had been robbed by the Democratic Party machines. They knew that, once again, the bullies in the schoolyard, the fabulously rich, movie-star-glamorous Kennedy clan had tormented the good kid: Richard Milhous Nixon.

But Nixon really was the good kid. Although he knew he had been robbed, he did not sue. He did not make a big national issue of the obvious fraud. He gave in to the bullies gracefully.

Despite all his pains, Mr. and Mrs. Kennedy never invited him to the White House. He was, as the English say, infra dig—beneath their dignity. LBJ made mocking, cruel fun of him. LBJ—of all people on the planet—called him a "chronic campaigner."

Mr. Nixon then made one of the worst mistakes of his life. He wanted badly to get back into politics at a high level. He wanted a launching pad for another try at the Oval Office.

What better launch pad than the governorship of California? RN was a native-born Californian. He had huge name recognition. He had pals who were immense names in the Golden State. The Democratic candidate for the office in Sacramento was Pat Brown, who looked like a human marshmallow. Brown had run up deficits. He had spent wildly on new construction of colleges and universities. He looked beatable.

He wasn't.

In fact, Nixon's opponent was well thought of in the state. He had powerful union support, especially among public service workers such as teachers. He was fantastically well heeled. He had at some point worked out an arrangement with the government of Indonesia, then Marxist and very much in Red China's orbit, about Indonesia's immense oil exports to the United States. In this deal, Mr. Brown was to personally get roughly fifty cents for each barrel of oil exported to the United States. That had amounted to many millions of dollars.

Once again, Richard Nixon, the poor boy from Whittier, was running against a plutocrat.

Probably worst of all for RN, there were still many in our state who recalled well his fight for the Senate against Helen Gahagan Douglas. They would never forgive RN for winning that election.

Some of these people were high powers in the state's media apparatus. The newspapers in the northern part of the state relentlessly mocked and belittled Nixon. The TV newscasts were scornful. They managed to convince many voters that RN was condescending to California after losing the big enchilada to JFK. (Interestingly enough though, the editorial board of the *Los Angeles Times*, by far the largest newspaper in the state, endorsed RN heartily in the election. As far as I can determine, these men and women endorsed RN in every one of his elections. Meanwhile, the "news hole," where reporters covered the day's news, or what they called news, was relentlessly hostile to RN.)

RN lost the election badly. The national media reported that RN was politically dead. The popular news "analysis" topic of the day was something along the lines of the political obituary of Richard Nixon.

Nixon did not help himself or his future by holding a press conference the next morning announcing that he had quit politics. That the media would no longer "have Dick Nixon to kick around." He then added the reason he was saying that: "Gentlemen, this will be my last press conference."

Very far from it. It was a sadly un-Nixonian performance. Of course, it turned out to be a long way from the truth.

CHAPTER THREE

THE *REAL* NIXON: HE COULD GET THINGS DONE, AND HE DID NOT STOP WORKING UNTIL THINGS GOT DONE

My brother-in-law, Melvin Epstein, a supersuccessful corporate lawyer in New York, recently told me, "Money is the best antidepressant." He's a lawyer, not a doctor, but I think he's onto something.

After his debacle in sunny California, RN entertained a number of offers of employment from major law firms, mostly in New York City. For the first time in his life, Richard Nixon would be in a position to make real money. His name was mud to the liberals and the beautiful people. But it was magic to firms papering state and local bond deals. Treasurers of states and counties and townships in the Midwest and the South and anywhere that did not heed the commands of the gorgeous people with lights in them knew the name Nixon. They did not know him as Tricky Dick.

They knew him as a still young man who could get the attention of powerful people in DC and on Wall Street. They knew him for what was in fact perhaps his greatest strength: He could get things done. He was a worker and did not stop until he got things done. Moreover, he did not consider working for corporations and state treasurers *infra dignitatem*.

After his loss in 1962 in the Golden State, Mr. Nixon went about his legal work successfully. He *greatly* raised the revenues of his new firm, Nixon, Mudge, Rose, Guthrie & Alexander. His pay went from nothing (so to speak) to a fabulous wage for the time—high six figures. He bought a spectacular home in San Clemente, a resort community right on the beach near the Marine base at Camp Pendleton.

The house was magnificent, with Spanish revival architecture and its own driving range and putting green overlooking the ocean. He also bought a modern dream house in Florida on an island connecting a spit of land called Key Biscayne.

He also bought a magnificent co-op on Fifth Avenue near Central Park. (It was at that time that he became friends with Donald Trump. Even then, in the 1960s, there were solemn "covenants" allowing members of the co-op to blackball a prospective owner/resident. At some buildings, RN was told that he was too "controversial" and would draw paparazzi and other undesirables to the building.)

(Trump, a newcomer to the ultralush, ultrasnobby, high-end co-op Manhattan real estate world, called RN and told him that RN would always be a welcome tenant at any of the Trump buildings. The Nixons never forgot. Julie told me this story in 2016 with a catch in her voice.)

(Just so you know, there are not just some but many high-end residential clubs in the United States that follow the same racist policies. No one in the media says a word about it. Why? That is *not* a tough question. Their bosses want to belong to the Chevy Chase Club. So do they.)

In any event, Dick Nixon had something he had never had before, the summum bonum of Americana: money. As anyone can tell you, it's a nice feeling to have.

This did not slow him down politically one little bit.

As detailed magnificently in Pat Buchanan's book *The Greatest Comeback*, Richard Nixon spoke, appeared at GOP gatherings, even backed candidates he did not esteem within the party to get himself to the top of the totem pole for the 1968 presidential election. The mobs, the riots, the looting, and the deeply split Democratic Party contributed mightily to RN's success.

Mr. Nixon was able to portray himself as the avatar of the good old days when General Eisenhower was running a peaceful, happy America, where if you sent your kids out to play, they would not come home reeking of marijuana and/or pregnant.

Although he was pitted against a mocking, hostile media, he rose in public esteem. The academics were solidly against him at the prestige summits of America, as always, and still he rose in public esteem. Just as an example, in the November 1968 elections, I voted by mail for RN, as I was a student at Yale Law School. My wife of only a few months was a student at Vassar College. She was a flaming antiwar voice. Her father, Col. Dale Denman Jr., had fought in bloody combat in Vietnam. He advised us to do anything we could to end the war. It was, he said, "a meat grinder" for U.S. forces, with no way he could see to win it. He was a big-time war hero; Silver Star in World War II and Bronze Star in Vietnam.

I took that to mean he wanted an RN victory, since Hubert H. Humphrey, the Democrat, had been LBJ's veep and had voiced support for LBJ repeatedly. My wife would not be moved. She had picked up the Yale vibe and had learned to dislike RN. If I was at a dinner party of my friends at YLS, as I often was, and said I was going to vote for RN, my table mates would assume I was joking.

Just to illustrate how intense the feelings on RN were, on Election Day 1968, my wife and I were driving down Elm Street in the middle of Yale, and my wife asked me if I thought Nixon had a chance. "I hope so," I said. "I voted for him."

My wife laughed. I told her I wasn't kidding. She was so upset that she told me (not asked me) to stop the car in the middle of the block. She got out of the car, slammed the door, and stormed out in protest of my vote.

By an amazing coincidence, she was wearing what was then in fashion, pink short shorts, which accentuated her beautiful legs. She also was carrying in her purse all her jewelry, preparatory for our scheduled trip back to DC to see my parents and hers.

Two young African American men stopped her on the sidewalk and tried to grab her purse away. She resisted them, and some great Yale undergrads came along and scared them off. When I got back to our apartment, my wife was able to laugh about it all.

(She is now the most ardent Richard Nixon fan and admirer on the planet.)

I wasn't kidding at all about hoping that Mr. Nixon won. That night in our tiny little apartment at 131 Howe Street, we went to sleep thinking that Humphrey had won. But by the morning it was clear that Mr. Nixon was able to eke out a victory against a genuinely great man, Hubert Horatio Humphrey, and he started assembling his team for governing this glorious America.

This is where my father comes into the picture.

My father was a solid genius who had gone to economics graduate school at the University of Chicago with gigantic figures as either students or professors who became more or less household names in the world of economics, including Frank Knight, Milton Friedman, Aaron Director, C. Lowell Harriss, and many others.

These were the days when the field had real economic rigor. It was not the days when "brilliant new theories" were sketched on the backs of napkins and then became gospel to major party presidential campaigns. These were the days when even a man named Franklin Delano Roosevelt took the subject seriously. Immense names in the field like John Maynard Keynes of Britain were listened to attentively at the Versailles conference as they hammered out a peace treaty for that horror of horrors, World War I.

My father had not been an academic after graduate school. Instead, he went into the U.S. Navy as an ensign to do his part in the biggest event in human history, World War II. As superheroes in the skies and on the seas and on the battlefield joined in with forces like the British Empire and the Red Army to defeat the Nazis and the Japanese, my father did basic training at Quantico, Virginia, then toiled in a small building in Washington, DC, on what was then a "top secret" project.

The top secret was that the United States planned to invade the good-sized and well-fortified Japanese-held island of Formosa, now called Taiwan. It turned out to be a hoax aimed at possible Japanese spies in DC. The plans my pop and others worked on were just to mislead the tenacious enemy into wasting his resources on Formosa. There never was any plan at all to invade Formosa. And there were no Japanese spies in DC. (Soviet spies, yes. Japanese, no.) But my pop did not know that. He toiled on the fake invasion plans. (How he knew anything about how invasions worked has always been a mystery to me.)

While he was doing that, still in his midtwenties, he wrote an essay about postwar economic policy. In those days, although it was clear that the Allies and the USSR were going to win the war, there was fear that after the war, the United States would sink back into a second or third phase of the Great Depression without the mammoth defense budgets that had been buoying up the economy from bust to ultraboom.

The essay was for a contest being sponsored by Pabst Brewing Company about the subject of postwar economics. Hundreds, maybe thousands of economists from all over the country entered the contest, for it had the first prize of $25,000, equal roughly to $375,000 in 2023. A lordly prize indeed.

My father wrote the essay that won first prize. For that he was famous for a time. In public prestige, he vaulted ahead of far older and more famous economists. He was even on the Groucho Marx radio quiz show *You Bet Your Life*.

He went from there to working for CED, the highest summit of corporate America for about twenty years, and then to Stanford and then to Brookings, a liberal think tank where he did not fit in at all. He was wondering what to do next when his friends and connections led to a major opportunity.

In the first month of RN's campaign, my father got a call from Milton Friedman (who really needs no introduction). Professor Friedman was a high honcho in RN's campaign. He knew that my father was a major talent at writing easy-to-understand essays about economics. Professor Friedman asked my father if he would write a series of essays for RN's campaign documents about fiscal and monetary policy: what was wrong with it under LBJ and how he would fix it.

My father was undecided about whether to do it, although why I have never understood. He politely asked my opinion. Like many smart people, he thought that because I was a lawyer, I might know something. Also, he knew I followed Nixon much more closely than he did. His questions were simple: Would it be a mistake for him to ally himself with a political figure as controversial as Richard Nixon? And could Nixon win?

I told him that it didn't really matter if RN won. By placing his advice and experience into the political pot during the '68 campaign, he would enrich the stew. His ideas would get some attention, and all economists want attention. Almost all human beings want attention.

And as to RN being controversial, I told him that I had never come across evidence that convinced me that there was any- thing seriously or even trivially bad about him. He had been the victim of hate RN groups all his life. But he was a patriot and a supersmart guy. He would do the nation a great deal of good.

Being an ultraradical at Yale, I knew for a fact that we (ultra- radicals) were largely in it for the fun and games. We had no solutions to any of the nation's problems. Neither did Mr. Hum- phrey, albeit an admirable man.

Nixon was a relatively fresh face (although he had been called "a chronic campaigner" by LBJ, a joke if ever there was one). He might have some fresh ideas. This was before the tax-and-spend— or rather, don't-tax-but-still-spend-generously—revolution brought about by the supply-side theory had swept over the proud Republican galleons, once models of fiscal, balanced budget rectitude.

Supply side was a name my father had given the theory. Supply-side theory was making progress, but it was still an outsider's idea. Ronald Reagan liked it, but George Bush, a pillar of Republicanism, called it "voodoo economics." Your humble servant made much of that in my turn in *Ferris Bueller's Day Off*.

Maybe by going back to some GOP founding principles about taxes and spending, RN might make a start at righting the ship of state generally—heavy emphasis on *might*.

The president was advised on economics primarily by Professor Friedman but also by a fine, intelligent man named Paul McCracken. Professor McCracken was chair of the Department of Economics at the University of Michigan. He was a superbly trained academic with decades of classroom and library experience. He had also, as my father often said, the finest personality and the best character of any human being he had ever met.

So to summarize, when my father asked my advice about whether he should throw in with the Nixon campaign, I said an unequivocal, "Yes, sir."

It turned out to be the right move, to put it mildly. My father had issued a book about economic policy: *The Fiscal Revolution in America: Policy in Pursuit of Reality*. It was a serious, heavyweight book. When Mr. Nixon won the election, there was a solid document to debate within the cabinet and in the nation's press generally.

(This was a different press from what we have today. It was a press that had some education besides in the ways of gossip and character assassination—although that soon changed.)

Mr. Nixon adopted the custom of having regular prayer services every Sunday morning. The officiating pastor rotated. So did the attendees, although they were always highly placed

White House officials or government honchos or friends of the First Family.

My father had, by Inauguration Day, January 20, 1969, been nominated to the president's preeminent group of economists, the three-person Council of Economic Advisers (CEA). He was a member, while Professor Paul McCracken was chair, and a capable man by the name of William Fellner joined my father as a member. Dr. Fellner was soon dismayed by the political world and went back to academe.

He was succeeded by the first woman member of the CEA. She was Professor Marina von Neuman Whitman. Among her many other credits, she was the daughter of one of the inventors of the desktop computer, John von Neuman. She was invariably pleasant, supersmart, and a thorough professional.

(I might mention here that the head of statistics gathering, Frances James, who led a large staff of statisticians and economists, was also a woman. No one ever made much of it or held a press conference about it. She just did her fine work in a quiet, systematic way. It used to be that women were just accepted as the *exact* equal of men in the Nixon White House, and no one made much of it.)

For some reason, perhaps because my father was a native of Washington, DC, and he would always be in DC over the weekend, he was invited to many of these prayer services. Mr. Nixon was kind enough to invite him to bring his family along.

So there we would be in the East Room of the White House listening to a minister, almost always a Protestant, leading prayer and song.

By that time, I was a third-year law student at Yale. I had long, hippie hair and a mustache and wore a wide-brimmed fedora, as hippies did in those days. There was a short receiving line after the service. Mr. and Mrs. Nixon were in the line. I don't recall who else was. I do recall that in the main hallway outside the East Room was a startlingly beautiful young woman with brown hair in a green wool coat. "A good Republican cloth coat," as Mr. Nixon might have said and did say in the famous Checkers speech in 1952, which saved his place on Ike's ticket.

The young woman was Julie Nixon, RN's daughter, and she was holding the leashes of the three Nixon dogs, King Timahoe, a spectacularly gorgeous Irish Setter; Pasha, a cute terrier; and Vicki, a poodle.

There were also numbers of what I took to be Executive Protective Service guards in plain clothes. In those days the EPS had taken over much of the duties of the Secret Service. They guarded high executive branch officials; some but not all diplomatic personnel; and the president and his family. That included Julie and her sister, Tricia, and, of course, Mr. and Mrs. Nixon.

As I passed down the receiving line, and as we approached Mr. and Mrs. Nixon, my father said to Mr. Nixon, "This is our son, Benjy. He's a law student at Yale. This is how they dress at Yale these days."

"And a great fan and admirer of yours, Mr. President, despite my clothes and hair," I added.

My mother, a well-educated economist, added, "A rose by any other name would smell as sweet."

Mrs. Nixon, who always had a great sense of humor, laughed appreciatively. Then they both bowled me over. Mrs. Nixon said to my mother, "I understand you're an economist. I was, too, briefly, during the war."

As she said it, I recalled reading it somewhere, but I was surprised that Mrs. Nixon knew that my mother was an economist. (Again, there was no bragging or screaming about either woman's professional credentials. Work was there to be done, and if a woman could do the job and wanted the job, she just did it, and public relations was secondary.) There was no time to talk about that issue. But I did take the time to say to the First Couple, "And we're all great dog fanciers, and you have some beautiful ones right there." I gestured toward Julie and the dogs as I said that.

"Go say hello," Mr. Nixon said, and I did. My wife, the same wife who had stalked off at Yale when I told her I had voted for Mr. Nixon a few months earlier, came with me.

"How are you?" I asked Julie. "I'm Ben Stein. My father over there is Herbert Stein. He's an economic adviser to your father. This is my wife, Alex. We've just come down from Yale for vacation. You've got some beautiful dogs there."

"I know who you are and who your father is," she said cheerily. "I think we're about the same age. I'm about to take these guys for a walk. Do you want to come along?"

And so we did, down the stairs and out onto the south-facing White House lawn. The EPS officers, whose names or even genders I do not even slightly recall, accompanied Julie, the dogs, my wife, and me.

I don't recall what we talked about, although my wife, who was about to graduate from Vassar College, and Julie, who had just graduated from Smith, talked about going to an all-women's college and its pluses and minuses.

We also talked about the near-uniform leftist bias at prestige colleges and universities at that time. "Why do you think that is?" Julie asked. That began a lifetime of Julie asking me questions that were far too deep for me to answer with any assurance.

"It's the fashion," my wife said.

"Eight years of Marxist indoctrination of the faculty," I said, "plus real resentment about the war in Vietnam."

"No one likes the war in Vietnam very much," Julie added in a serious tone.

The walk was extremely brief, and then we all went our separate ways. Alex and I could hardly believe what we had just done. Let's face it: the White House is an important place. The First Daughter is a somebody. And she had just invited us to be her friends and walking companions right off the bat. Instead of walking around Georgetown shopping for posters, as Alex and I might ordinarily have done, or maybe driving along the Rock Creek Parkway, an amazingly beautiful urban viewscape, we were walking with Julie Eisenhower at the White House.

And her father and mother had treated us as if we were family. It was a euphoric feeling.

It was also an educational feeling. Here was Richard M. Nixon, hated and vilified by most of the people in Alex's and my world, called the most horrible names in the "prestige" media, treated as if he were Richard III in Shakespeare's play, behaving like a character out of *The Adventures of Ozzie and Harriet*. Here was the Tricky Dick who had unseated the saintly Helen Gahagan Douglas, making us a member of the Nixon household the first moment he met us. (I doubt if he recalled meeting us at campaign train stops roughly twenty years before.) *The Adventures of Ozzie and Harriet* was a situation comedy of the 1950s and early 1960s that showed the absolute essence of ordinary, unpretentious middle-class life in small-town America. If he were just playing a part, the part of Ozzie Nelson, he played it incredibly well. To say that he was a gifted performer would have been putting it mildly. Was it possible that what we had seen that day was the real Nixon and that the media image of him was wrong?

But then where did either image come from?

That's what lay in store for me to learn—or at least to poke around the edges.

CHAPTER FOUR

THE MAN INSIDE THE NIXON MASK

Time passed, as it always does until it stops. I was about to graduate from Yale Law School. I needed to find a job. I could not live forever on student loans or my earnings as the director of the Yale Law School Film Society. Jobs were generally allocated on the basis of grades and learned writing.

My grades were good but by no means superlative. I had good extracurricular activities, especially doing volunteer work for poor, mostly Black people in the housing projects of New Haven.

I had done a huge amount of work fundraising for a new Black self-help group called the Black Panthers. This entity supposedly raised money for giving out free, nourishing breakfasts to indigent Black children in a neighborhood called the Hill. This was a groundbreaking effort, for a superwhite, superprestigious group of boys and girls to raise money to feed poor Black children in New Haven. We had gotten publicity and awards for our work. Far from using our skills to help the rich pay fewer taxes, we were feeding fatherless Black children in a slum.

That's what we thought, anyway. Sadly, it turned out that the Black Panthers were largely a criminal enterprise dealing drugs and death. How much of the money we raised supposedly for scrambled eggs and milk and cereal went for .223 ammo we will never know.

However, in the spring of 1970, people who hired lawyers did not care about the Black Panthers or the free-breakfast program. As always, they wanted lawyers who could make the rich richer. Plus, I had worked two summers as a law clerk at a major Washington law firm, then called Arnold, Fortas & Porter. For one summer, I worked at a Wall Street firm called Reavis & McGrath.

My main takeaway from those firms was of lawyers screaming at each other and working long hours to (again) make the rich richer. Not something I wanted to spend my life doing.

I wanted to work helping poor people or enforcing laws controlling bad corporate actors. There were such entities. One was the Office of Legal Services (OLS) of the federal government. Its main headquarters was in Washington, DC, and in a great neighborhood. It supervised a huge network of federally paid lawyers who provided free legal services to the poor.

But those jobs were hard to come by. A law grad needed something special in his or her résumé. Something beyond the Black Panthers. What would that something be for me? I had written a long paper about changes in the commission structure for stock trading. It was fine but not enough. I needed something *big*.

For all eternity, YLS had selected its graduation valedictory speaker on the basis of who had the highest grades in the class.

But in the revolutionary days of 1969 and 1970, we changed the grading system. No longer were there numerical or letter grades, like 86 or B+. Instead, the grades were *pass, high pass, honors*. And *fail*. Obviously, not a huge change, but it was something. There were also sometimes (not always for sure) little essays by the teachers about the students, such as "Benjy Stein has been a fine and outspoken student and understands the need for more social justice in the laws of contracts."

The valedictorian for the class of 1970 was selected by the votes of the graduating class. I was a popular student because I was one of the only students who dared talk back to the teachers, some of whom were outright bullies and condescending snobs. Most were kind, brilliant, thoughtful men and women whom we adore and pray for night and day, even now.

On one occasion, I became, in one class session, a superstar of the age of rebellion. The teacher in antitrust, a Mr. Gordon Spivak, was doing his usual sneering routine.

In the worst kind of "Socratic method" teaching, he asked questions to which there was simply no answer. Example: How many people have to be given a certain antibiotic before there is an antitrust issue? There is no answer to that kind of question. Mr. Spivak asked for someone to answer the question.

I raised my hand, and he called on me. "What's your name?" he asked.

"You can call me Benjy," I said to him.

"No. I mean your last name," he asked peremptorily.

"Sir, you can just call me Benjy," I repeated.

"All right, Benjy," he said with contempt so thick and gooey, you could have heated it and used it to sauté a steak. "How many people have to be given a certain antibiotic for there to be an antitrust issue?"

"Mr. Spivak, sir, there is no precise answer to that question, as you, above all, would know. It just depends on the mood of the judge that day and what the media is calling for."

"So you don't have an answer?" he asked mockingly.

"No, sir, there is no precise answer. This is just one of your typical unanswerable Socratic method questions. We both know it. Why don't you just tell us that, and let's go on to the next case."

"I want to know your answer," Mr. Spivak demanded. "I need to know your answer."

"Sir, with the greatest possible respect, you have my answer. And if you don't stop asking these bullying questions, I am going to take my clothes off in class and start reading the names of the Vietnam War dead."

At this point, the class was exploding with laughter. The smartest student in my class, Duncan Kennedy, who was later to become a superstar teacher at Harvard Law School and an early exponent of critical legal studies, was laughing wildly and slapping me on the back.

Mr. Spivak got red in the face, gathered up his papers, and stalked out of the room. He resigned soon thereafter and went down to New York to practice antitrust law. Several years later there was an article about him in a law magazine that said he was the most highly paid antitrust lawyer in the world. Soon after that, a mutual friend told me that he was still cursing my name, although mixed with gratitude that I had helped him make so much money.

Almost immediately, my fellow students elected me valedictorian of my class. There it was: my big credential.

Back to my 1969–70 job quest . . . In life, appearance is extremely important, and connections are vital. I drew liberally upon both to get my job serving the poor.

I altered my appearance. I still had long hippie hair and a mustache, but they were much moderated. I stopped wearing tie-dyed T-shirts. I gave up my precious purple tie-dyed bell-bottomed trousers and their accompanying purple heavily designed belts. I even gave up my sandals.

It's been fifty-two years now, and I still miss it all. It is a major part of life to "look cool." I had managed to "look cool," and now, for work, for a job, I was giving it all away. From camos to Brooks Brothers in one fell swoop.

But that would certainly not be enough to do it. In life, connections are life and death. I had plenty. Yale Law School had immense assets. We had fine teachers, a fine library, fabulously good art and architecture, even a superb dining hall. (When I first entered Yale, the dining hall had waiters in livery who took our orders and brought us our scrambled eggs on fine china with real metal, maybe even silver utensils.)

So I had my target job at the Office of Legal Services, a famous father, lots of faculty at Yale who agreed with me about Mr. Spivak, and lots of recommendations from them.

Thus, just a few days after graduation, I set off to DC to begin my job at the OLS.

People are heavily influenced by their surroundings. The OLS was in a plain office building. Its floors were almost all rented by government agencies. They were staffed by intelligent but sad-looking officials. One of the myths about bureaucrats is that they are stupid. Some are, but most of the ones I worked for were intelligent and hardworking. Generally, they are not entrepreneurial in a society that worships wealth. But they are often impressive human beings.

The men and women at the OLS were no exception. The entire staff at the OLS was intelligent and disciplined. From the secretaries (there were no computers in those days) to the boss—a very aggressive, recently deceased Terry Lenzner—the workers earned their keep.

But the work was boring and repetitive. Instead of going out into the field, as one might say, we were processing the reports of the field offices: how many cases they undertook, what kinds of cases they were, how many cases they won, and how many they lost. Plus, we needed to know their payrolls, the legal résumés of their law staff, and their pay and benefits.

I did this "work" in a windowless office that I shared with a man whose name I do not recall. I'm not sure I ever knew his name.

I complained about the situation to my father. He was at the Old Executive Office Building, generally considered part of the White House. His office was a palace. It was an immense room with a working fireplace and glorious bay windows overlooking the Washington Monument and the Ellipse. He had two satin-covered couches and a big conference table. The floors in the Old EOB were black-and-white marble rectangles. Floors were connected by splendid spiral staircases. It was an artwork of architecture and decorations and luxury. That hypnotized me. Again, men and women are greatly influenced by their surroundings, and my dreary rooms at the OLS made me feel dreary. The palace at Seventeenth and Pennsylvania NW made me feel elevated.

Now, life is largely about who you know and who your parents are. I often came up from the OLS to have lunch with my father at the White House Mess. It was a small dining room where

only high-ranking members of the White House staff and cabinet members were allowed to eat. My father was allowed to eat
there. He was also the best father there has ever been, and so he
invited me to eat there with him frequently.

The White House Mess (so called because it was officially
a navy mess hall) was in the West Wing of the White House.
The biggest of big shots passed by it all day long. At one point,
probably in 1971, as I was walking out of the White House with
my pop, there was some considerable commotion. It turned out
that Mr. Nixon was about to pass by, with Bob Haldeman, the
White House chief of staff and a much-feared presence, in tow.

(Some days after that, when I was eating with my father in
the mess, I saw Mr. Haldeman eating with someone, maybe
John Ehrlichman, chairman of the Domestic Policy Council. I
said, referring to Bob Haldeman, "He looks like a jolly fellow.")

("Yes," said my pop, "a jolly steel buzz saw.")

(In 1976, before he went off to prison for completely fraudulent crimes, when I had moved to Los Angeles and Bob lived
there as well, I took him for lunch several times at the old La
Scala in Beverly Hills. He could not have been more charming.
We had a substantial correspondence while he was at Lompoc.)

Anyway, as Mr. Nixon passed by, looking extremely intent,
probably about the nightmare of Vietnam, he greeted my father
by saying, "How are you, Herb?"

"Fine, thank you," said my father. "Do you remember my
son, Ben?"

"Of course," said the president of the United States. "Julie tells
me you are quite a dog lover."

"God bless you, Mr. President," I replied. "God bless you," I
repeated. "You carry a heavy load."

He patted me on the shoulder and replied, "You bet."

Then he rushed by onto West Executive Avenue and up the stairs to his "hideaway office" in the Old EOB.

My head was spinning as I went back to the OLS. "I have to get back there somehow," I thought to myself.

And then, as if a wizard had struck with his magic cane, when I came back from heaven to work at the Office of Legal Services, I had a call from my father. He told me to come down to the Old EOB again on the double.

I did, and he was sitting in his palace of an office smoking one of the innumerable cigarettes that eventually killed him. In a nutshell, my father asked me if I wanted to work on the White House staff, although in a minor way.

Robert Brown, a supersmart, successful businessman from North Carolina, was special assistant to the president for minority affairs. This encompassed a wide range of duties. Just as an example, one of the tasks was to make sure that Black-owned businesses were allowed and even encouraged to bid on federally funded projects ranging from highway construction in rural areas to a skyscraper building in downtown Charlotte.

He was also to monitor compliance with court-ordered public school integration, especially in the Deep South.

His office was understaffed. He had mentioned to Bob Haldeman that he needed someone young and good at statistics to help carry the load. Bob Haldeman had mentioned this to some officials in the presence of my father. And that group included Mr. Nixon. Incredibly, Mr. Nixon remembered that at some point, when parents were bragging, my father had mentioned that his son was especially good at statistics gathering and summarizing.

From this had come an offer for me to work part time at the Old EOB under Bob Brown. The job would pay nothing (literally nothing). But Terry Lenzner would let me go from his large bureaucracy for three evenings a week and still pay me full time. And I would trudge happily up to the Old EOB and do my work.

I was happy about every single detail of the project. It did mean that I usually had to come in late and work on weekends to get it all done, but that was my pleasure. I got to see the data up close and personal that told me how well the RN administration was doing in integrating the last of the holdout Dixie schools.

As far as I could tell, the White House and the Justice Department were really cracking the whip. The percentage of students in the Deep South who were still attending all-Black or all-white schools had fallen from roughly 20 percent in early 1969 to roughly 5 percent by 1971. This was a big jump.

It told me that real progress was being made and that the vile allegations that RN was in his heart a segregationist were false. From the first to the last time, I would discover that negative allegations about Mr. Nixon were almost always demonstrably false.

I also saw that Nixon administration programs for aiding the Black men and women who wanted to break into business were going well. To be sure, there was little yelling and screaming and no bullying about this progress. It was not a ploy to get votes. It was just the way Mr. Nixon felt about the world. He did not believe that all Americans were equal in every way. He did not believe that Americans in general, of whatever skin color, were equal in abstract reasoning, mathematics, basketball, running, or musical ability or language, just for example. But he did intensely believe that all Americans should have equal rights under the law.

Even though he was an anti–big government, small-town Southern California Republican, he believed that the overwhelming might of the federal government should be employed from time to time to give Black Americans a leg up to make certain their rights were not being held down by local lawmakers or law enforcers who clearly would use delaying dances to keep Blacks well behind whites in access to equal education and/or accommodation.

He knew history, and he knew government. He knew that even after the Thirteenth, Fourteenth, and Fifteenth Amendments had been enacted, supposedly giving Black former slaves completely equal rights under the law, the reality was different. He knew (as he often later told me) that the "good old boys" in southern and border states and even in the western United States were able to use devices to greatly restrict the rights and powers of the Black man and woman.

As I read in a memo that he sent to Bob Brown, my boss at the White House, "once the Blacks get the right to vote," everything will change. At that point, "the Blacks will be the bosses of the local authorities, and little by little, the local bosses will discover that the Blacks had always been their best friend and that they loved the Blacks." (This is most definitely not a verbatim quote.)

As I have already noted, Mr. Nixon was a fan and reader of the great Milton Friedman, the Nobelist explicator of the truth that capitalism and freedom were indispensable partners of each other. He had read and believed that the right to vote was a valuable commodity. Once the Black person had it in abundance, his or her whole position in society would change drastically, at least in reality, if not in the way the powers that be perceived it.

So as I worked my job for Bob Brown, I learned considerable details about Mr. Nixon's positions on civil rights and about Blacks and other persons of color in America in general.

I did not by any means work closely with Mr. Nixon at this time. I only saw him infrequently, usually as he happened to be walking down the immense stairs from the Old EOB to the White House. I was endlessly amazed at his memory and his friendship. Although my position was a minor one at best, he always remembered my name. He always asked to be remembered to my mother. He remembered her by her first name as well and was well aware that my mother was endlessly churning out letters to the editor at the *Washington Post* defending RN and the Republicans generally. Amazingly, he was familiar with what each of these letters—the ones that were printed, at least—said.

How he could have done that seems, even after half a century, impossible. And yet there it was.

I remember that each time I saw him, I thought that there was another man inside a Nixon mask. That man was a Lord Byron or a Keats or a Shelley. He was a poet, and when his last hour at the White House came at the hands of the press, he did not read statistics about how when he entered office in January of 1969, there were five hundred thousand young Americans fighting and many dying in Vietnam and now there were almost none. He did not talk about how when he entered the Oval Office as a conservative Republican, there were hundreds of

Deep South school districts mandatorily segregated by race, and now there were almost none.

He did not mention that the endless riots were over and that the streets were peaceful again (largely thanks to his own self-sacrifice).

Instead, he talked about love and read a poetic passage about young Theodore Roosevelt and the catastrophe of his losing his young bride. He was a poet wrapped inside a politician. There was no Tricky Dick. Instead, there was a sensitive, artistic Richard Nixon inside and a shell of a tough, shrewd guy outside.

That was how I saw things, and I think that Mr. Nixon knew that I realized that about him almost instinctually from day one.

In the meantime, while the world turned, I came and went to the White House to do a bit of work and hang with my father, another subject that preoccupied RN when we met, which, again, was infrequent.

He often asked how my father was and what he was working on. Usually the answer was the *Annual Economic Report of the President.* This was a lengthy tome about the economy. In those years, it had many chapters in my father's superbly clear prose. These discussed economic growth, unemployment, trade, tax policy, and fiscal and monetary policies in a serious way. He wrote them in longhand on a pad of lined paper. In those days, there were no personal computers.

There were no comic books and no discussion of racism. There was a great deal of data but no exhortation about the unfortunate situation of the Blacks and what measures were being undertaken to help.

Then as now, the CEA was well aware of the problems in Black America. Then as now, no one had any idea of how to help it except to throw money at it.

Following the chapters were hundreds of pages of statistics about almost anything that had to do with economics. These were prepared by the staff of the CEA, a group of mostly young economists and statisticians under the watchful eye of Frances James.

Working with slide rules and Marchant and Monroe calculators and avalanches of paper work from the various government agencies, the staff prepared a genuine encyclopedia of what was going on and what had gone on in the economy. In more recent years, this section of the report has shrunk.

Mr. Nixon, I am morally certain, did not read much of those endless columns of numbers. He probably did read the opening chapter, below which his signature appeared. This was mostly cheerleading and sometimes regrets but not serious analysis. Still, he seemed to be aware of every single person on the staff and what he or she was doing. Impressive.

He also was endlessly bemused by the truth that both my father and I were working at the White House at the same time. He spoke briefly about what it would have meant to him if his father could have worked with him when he was a young lawyer and politician. He noted with happiness that his father had lived to see him become vice president under Dwight Eisenhower and to stand with him on the inaugural platform in 1953.

"A man's connection with his father is not just important," he said. "It's vital."

After a year or so of work at the OLS and the White House, a close friend persuaded me that I should not be doing what I was doing. Instead, I should be a trial lawyer. After all, I was (and am) a lawyer. And after all, if I were ever going to make any real money, it would have to be as a lawyer and not as a bureaucrat.

I won't go into the tale of my work as a trial lawyer for the Federal Trade Commission in 1971–72 in their Bureau of Consumer Protection in any depth. It was hard work. My opponents on the main case I worked on, about a soft drink called Hi-C, were experienced and tough. I admired them. The case against their client, Coca-Cola Company, should never have been brought. I was against it but was overruled.

My colleagues at the FTC were brilliant but, like me, inexperienced. The FTC basically had no support staff, while our opponents were drowning in help of a competent nature. My work at the FTC was grinding me to a nub.

It also meant that I had to give up my work at the White House. That really hurt.

By the grace of God and the help of Mr. Kauffman, I got an adjunct job teaching about the political and social messages of Hollywood movies at American University (AU) in Washington, DC. I taught for three semesters about Film and War, Film and Revolution, and Film and Economics. The classes were wildly popular. By the third semester there, I had 360 students, the largest class ever at AU.

The students loved me so much that they stood, cheered, clapped, and whistled when I walked into the lecture hall, before I even started to speak. Those were the happiest days of my life and still are.

Despite that happiness, the pressure from trial law over the Hi-C case was way too much for me. It was all tension and overwork. I wound up drastically ill with colitis, took an extended leave, and by a great stroke of luck, by September of 1972, found myself teaching at the most beautiful campus in the world, the glens and forests of the University of California Santa Cruz (UCSC).

Just before I left DC for UCSC, late one night, possibly in June of 1972, I saw on the local DC news that five men had been arrested for breaking into the headquarters of the Democratic National Committee at the Watergate complex at Virginia and New Hampshire Avenues NW. No one knew why they did it or who sent them. To this day, no one knows what they were looking for. My guess then and now was that they were sent by a Democratic "sleeper" exactly for them to be caught and traced back to Nixon's men and thus to embarrass Nixon. It did not work in the 1972 election, but it worked extremely well for the Democrats afterward.

I got an eerie vibe from the story but went off to California nevertheless.

CHAPTER FIVE

CALIFORNIA PART 1: A BIG CHANGE IN MY LIFE

In 1972, the campus at UCSC was magnificent beyond what the normal mind can envision. It was a roughly fifteen-thousand-acre plot, formerly a granite quarry with surrounding redwood forests. Thanks to the vision of the leaders of the Golden State, it had been transformed into a university campus. It was modeled on the order of my law school alma mater, Yale, in that it was divided into several separate colleges, each specializing in something: marine biology, history, science, and my college, College V, which was the arts college.

My specialty in that college was the implicit—that is, not openly stated—social and political message of certain famous movies. I had been gifted with being allowed to study film at Yale in the graduate school of drama (even though I was a law student) under the legendary film critic and supernice man Stanley Kauffman. In his class, I developed a theory that films have various hidden messages—pro–free enterprise, Marxist, mixed, patriotic, subversive, and everything and anything in between.

These were not openly political movies like *Mr. Smith Goes to Washington* but movies supposedly about nonpolitical subjects, like Vittorio De Sica's *Bicycle Thieves*.

Mr. Kauffman liked the thoughts so much that he advised me to drop law school and go to Hollywood and write for it and about it. (In a way, I did.)

So, again, while I was working at the OLS and at the EOB, I was also teaching two nights at American University in Washington, DC, to large and enthusiastic mobs of students. (Again, those were the happiest days of my life.) The classes were widely discussed in the world of film studies, and, again, I was able to get a small job at UCSC, the world's most glorious campus.

But the campus was also utterly politically one sided. The 1972 election had called forth roughly fifteen hundred ballots on the campus. Of these, all but two were for the Democrat George McGovern. The two for Mr. Nixon were from me and a Vietnam War vet. The morning after the election, some students created a giant swastika in the dining hall. I ordered them to take it down. They did, but they complained to the head of the college, James B. Hall. He wrote back a shockingly anti-Semitic comment about me to them.

In it, he railed against the "big-money eastern types like $tein." Yes, he spelled it with a dollar sign. He sent the letter to the students who had made the giant swastika. They Xeroxed the letter and circulated the copies around the campus.

I was furious and marched into Professor Hall's office to speak to him. My path was blocked by Mr. Hall's immensely tall, frighteningly angry secretary, Ms. Clarnelle Strandberg. I had experienced nothing but trouble from her since I got to campus in August. She was always in a bad mood. She also had a tall, stocky, somewhat scary-looking son who wandered around the College V campus, especially at night. His name was Ed Kemper.

Rumor had it that Ed had murdered his grandparents by setting their home afire while they were sleeping when he was a young teenager or maybe even earlier.

California being what it is, he was soon out free and easy. Meanwhile, there was a blood-curdling spate of kidnappings, rapes, and murders by strangulation of co-eds around campus.

Finally, Clarnelle let me in to see Professor Hall. He was sitting in his chair clipping his nails as I told him of my outrage. He blithely told me that he always wrote his *S*s as dollar signs and that he had nothing further to say.

I told him I would resign and leave UCSC at the end of the quarter unless he apologized for his anti-Semitic gesture. Clarnelle, who had sat in on the colloquy, guffawing, led me out.

Sure enough, he did not apologize. By that time, I was also teaching a class in political and civil rights under the Constitution at Cowell College. I hated to leave both colleges, but I had said I would, and I did. Early one morning, I packed my meager belongings into my pitiful Subaru and headed to the San Jose International Airport to fly back to DC.

My mother, God rest her soul, met me at Dulles International Airport, and so began a big change in my life.

I returned to the FTC, which had kindly allowed me to be on a paid leave of absence while I was at UCSC. They took me back and started me working on questionable advertisements for the so-called Mark Eden bust developer. I was in the smallest office in a dreary building that had once housed the great *Washington Evening Star* newspaper.

The building was in a neighborhood so dingy that homeless men urinated against the walls of its front entrance in broad daylight.

I hated it.

Meanwhile, events had taken an interesting turn back at UCSC. The Santa Cruz Police Department had gotten a call from my old neighbor, Ed Kemper. He wanted to show them something.

The police came over, and Ed genially showed them to his mother's bedroom closet. There, leaning against the wall, was the headless body of my nemesis, Clarnelle. Ed Kemper explained to the police that he was the number-one Santa Cruz co-ed rapist and killer. (There were two others operating at the same time.)

His mother, clever detective that she was, had suspected her little boy had something to do with the murdered co-eds. She questioned him. He responded by murdering her and defiling her body, and then he called the police.

In case you're wondering, he's still in prison. Even in California, there are limits. He's on various true-crime shows often.

He is said to be a model prisoner.

I had reported the whole zany episode with J. B. Hall to my father, then chairman of the CEA. He had written a letter to his friend, Governor Ronald W. Reagan. Mr. Reagan as governor was also chair of the University of California board of regents.

Governor Reagan wrote to my father that he was disgusted but not surprised by what Professor Hall had done. He had years of experience with academics in our glorious state. He convened a subcommittee of the regents to look into things. Professor Hall assured them that he always wrote his Ss as dollar signs. The subcommittee, all UC faculty members, said they believed him.

But they suggested that in view of his heavy workload and his advanced age, it might be time for him to retire. He did.

It's incredible what having a well-connected father can do for a man or woman.

CHAPTER SIX

PLENTY TO FEAR: MEDIA LYNCH MOB AND THE
MAN WHO SAVED THE CHILDREN OF ISRAEL

And back in Washington, that little burglary at the Watergate had turned into a big thing. Soon after the Metropolitan Police Department conveniently received a call that a door at the Watergate garage that was usually locked had black masking tape that kept the tongue suppressed and the door from being locked, a cascade began.

The Watergate burglars were found to be Cuban immigrants in the United States and employees of President Nixon's reelection entity, CRP (the Committee to Re-elect the President), or CREEP, as Nixon's enemies call it. Then a line ran from the regular staff into CREEP, including my former neighbor in the EOB, a mysterious-looking man named E. Howard Hunt.

From there the lines ran in all directions.

The media ran wild with stories that Richard Nixon had personally directed a variety of illegal acts against the Democrats during the '72 campaign and, in fact, for all eternity.

Top White House aides were summoned into congressional hearing rooms for grilling. Men who had elevated statuses in the White House and therefore in the nation generally became pariahs and gangsters.

I was still toiling away at my tiny little desk at the FTC, investigating the Mark Eden bust developer. My former next-door neighbor when I was a child, Carl Bernstein, was writing gigantically followed stories about Watergate and had become a media superstar, along with his comrade, Bob Woodward. We had been close friends forever, and although I believed his writing was mistaken, I liked him and still do. Carl was later to play an extremely important and helpful role in my life: he introduced me to his literary agent, David Obst.

I had begun some months before writing op-eds defending RN and especially railing against what seemed to me to be the most constitutionally invalid persecution of Bob Haldeman. He had basically been indicted, tried, and convicted by Congress without even a shred of legal due process.

Those op-eds were published in major newspapers, including the *Washington Post* (where I had been a copyboy in a summer job in 1963 or 1964 and had written my first published articles), the *New York Times*, and the *Wall Street Journal*. They were uniformly pro-Nixon.

I pointed out that insofar as I had seen, no major or even minor crimes had been committed by Mr. Nixon or by anyone high in his administration.

The whole screaming and shrieking reminded me of a lynch mob far more than a reasoned exercise of law by the greatest nation in the world. The liberal press was positively giddy with blood lust against RN, and I saw no reason for it grounded in good sense or fact.

FDR had famously said in 1933, apropos the Great Depression, that "we have nothing to fear but fear itself." That was wildly incorrect. There was plenty to fear, especially a drastically harmful monetary policy that was crushing the U.S. economy and workers.

In the case of Watergate, as far as I could see, the only cause for hysteria was the adrenaline rush from hysteria itself. The media was on an Orwellian "two-minute hate," only it was lasting months and years.

Hate can organize your thoughts. It can push away feelings of responsibility for one's own faults and failings. It's going to kill the hater in the end, but for the time being, it's like being high on a drug. And the media was high on the drug of hating Nixon. Newsreel film footage of Nazi rallies against the Jews gives you an idea of what was happening in DC.

But there were rays of light. In those days, newspapers printed articles on the op-ed page by writers they disagreed with and with points of view that they wholly disagreed with. So I could write in print and discuss on TV that the Watergate victims had been denied constitutional protections, had not been shown to have done anything clearly illegal, and yet were being lynched in the media and were almost certain to be lynched in fact.

At that time and in that place, few and far between were the writers who were able to write a clear essay with legal citations backing the Nixon White House and especially Mr. Nixon himself.

Thus, my articles came to the attention of high officials in the White House. They shared them with other high officials in the Nixon White House. In particular, Peter M. Flanigan, the impossibly handsome, impossibly smart, impossibly rich, impossibly brave (World War II Navy fighter pilot), impossibly charming aide for foreign trade at the White House, who was a great pal of my parents, read them and liked them.

He spoke to Ray Price, head of the speech-writing staff, and to Dave Gergen, who was just under Mr. Price. They also spoke to Pat Buchanan, the legendary Nixon colleague, and to Len Garment, the White House counsel. They noted that there was an extra office in the speech-writing suite of offices because the greatest speechwriter of them all, Bill Safire, had recently left to write a column for the *New York Times* op-ed page. (Another thing that could not happen today.)

All these people, especially Safire and Garment, were great pals of my parents. For that reason as well as for my pro-Nixon articles, these kind people offered me a job in the EOB. Again, the EOB was and still is considered a part of the White House.

The kind people at the FTC, especially my brilliant and smart boss, Gerald Thain, agreed to "lend" me to the WH staff for a few months to see if I worked out as a speechwriter.

In late November 1973, I reported to a tiny office at the EOB to be briefed by my immediate boss, Dave Gergen. Dave was and is a wildly tall, florid-faced man with impressive credentials: a Yale BA and a Harvard LLB. He's fantastically smart. He appeared in my tiny shoebox of an office with a beautiful young woman named Anne Morgan, who was chief of research for the speech-writing staff. (She went on to become a successful lawyer.)

In what turned out to be a practical joke, they asked me what I wanted in my office. I said I would like a couch long enough to take naps in, since I understood I would be working long hours and might need to rest, and also that I would like a TV so that I could watch the news and soap operas. I told them I had found that I could get a taste of the national mood by following the soaps.

They scoffed at my requests, but within a few hours, I had a lovely office with just what I wanted. They had been doing some sort of "hazing" earlier.

My office was in the middle of a suite of offices. To my immediate south was a brilliant man named John R. Coyne Jr., who had recently been moved there from the staff of the departed "Ted" Agnew. To my immediate north was the large office of a mustachioed genius named Aram Bakshian Jr. Although I did not recall it immediately, I had met Aram when we were both in high school. We had debated public versus private schools. His knowledge of history and music was stupefyingly impressive. He never finished college, and I have never met a college grad who knew as much as he did. (He passed away from a cruel pancreatic cancer as this book was being written.)

Immediately, I was given difficult messages to write. These were not speeches but missives to Congress accompanying proposed legislation, often about enormous subjects such as universal health care for all Americans, which Richard Nixon was the first to propose to Congress. To compose such a message required the input of many different cabinet-level departments, revisions by the Office of Management and Budget, and the control of the final draft by Dave Gergen; Ray Price; John Ehrlichman, the head of the Domestic Policy Council; and Donald Rumsfeld, my old boss at the OLS and eventually the replacement for Bob Haldeman as White House chief of staff.

Finally, it required the input of Mr. Nixon himself.

All of this was an enormously complex and time-consuming process. I was staggered that the powers that be trusted me to be involved at a high level.

As Gergen explained, I was their only writer who had serious training in law and also in economics. That qualified me for many tasks. Plus, my father had the reputation of being a brilliant man, and the higher-ups rightly assumed that I would bring anything complicated to his attention.

The first comprehensive energy plan was also a project assigned to me. This was a plan to produce immense amounts of energy by "clean" methods such as solar power and the harnessing of wind in many areas of the nation. Amazingly, it also called for the use of waves in the shoreline of America. This method seemed like science fiction to me, but Nixon was always a forward thinker.

As I look back on those endless days and nights working on such immense subjects, I can hardly believe it really happened.

The whole situation felt unreal. I would be working until midnight or later, along with other writers and researchers. Then I would call Pat, my close friend—really my girlfriend, since I was then divorced—to come get me in my little blue Subaru. She would appear a few minutes later with our dog, a perfect Weimaraner named Mary Margaret of Santa Cruz. The dog was a thoroughbred we had bought when we lived in Santa Cruz. No creature on earth was more beautiful, faithful, and loving.

The Executive Protective Service guards all had mad crushes on Pat. So they let her in with our dog. The dog ran down the magnificent black-and-white marble-tiled floors to my office, barking and howling. Then she would find my office, leap up onto my lap, and start to lick me.

After a few weeks of this, Don Rumsfeld issued a staff directive that no one except the president was to bring any dogs into the White House complex. The barking and the loud clicking noise of Mary's nails on the tile were distracting, as Mr. Rumsfeld explained.

I think I would be deceptive if I did not acknowledge that as of this time, in late '73 and early '74, I was quite convinced that the manipulation of public opinion by the mass media and Congress, plus the timidity of the GOP in Congress, meant that RN's presidency was in desperate shape, at best.

My father and I often took long walks after lunch around the back (south) White House lawn and discussed the situation. Neither of us could see any way out unless the congressional GOP threw themselves into the fight. Characteristically, this was something that they would not do. We often wondered how many of us at the White House would be caught in the dragnet. Dave Gergen had already threatened me that if I was caught outside my office during the day for any reason, I would be called before the Watergate grand jury.

How my work was in any way related to the alleged criminal acts called under the cover name of "Watergate" was never clear. Dave Gergen was a great one for practical jokes.

But I should also acknowledge that my affection for RN was so great that I would have worked for him even if it meant a certain prison sentence. There were many reasons for this affection.

First and least important, President Nixon had ennobled, so to speak, my father and mother. Instead of their being your ordinary high-end brainos, even well-paid ones, as my father was, my parents were invited to embassy parties on heavy-duty elegant paper. They were invited to the queen's birthday parties at the British embassy.

They and their children were invited to use the White House box at the Kennedy Center. That's a room with eight chairs and its own bathroom in a great spot in the auditorium. They could use the incredibly lavish presidential retreat in the Catoctin Mountains, the so-called Camp David. It had a swimming pool heated to about ninety degrees. It was like floating in paradise. It was the kind of resort that one could only dream of. It had new, shiny Ethan Allen furniture in lavishly bright, cheerful "cabins" designed for visitors like Winston Churchill or Anthony Eden.

Much more important, my father, who had been a lone intellectual among supersuccessful rich businessmen almost all his life, was now part of a *team* of men and women, highbrows like Pat Moynihan and Henry Kissinger and tough guys like Haldeman. Of different religious and social backgrounds, to be sure, but all ideologically committed to a free-enterprise America whose government was led by Richard M. Nixon—who called my father and mother by their first names. They called him Mr. Nixon, even when they were talking about him at their home, far from the White House.

For my father, being a member of a team, the "first team," as John R. Coyne called it, was intoxicating.

My parents were never before or after as happy as when they belonged to this team. And never as sad as the day he resigned.

Second and by far more important, Richard Nixon was the best friend the Jews of the world had ever had.

Perhaps someone is going to read this and note that the White House transcripts reveal that Mr. Nixon used derogatory terms in referring to us Jews. That has never bothered me at all.

On October 6, 1973, the earth opened up, and the chaos of a second Holocaust was upon the children of Israel. Israel had fought three major wars since its independence in May 1948. They had won them all, against the odds. With little more than sticks and stones, Israel and its citizen army largely of death camp survivors had beaten the well-equipped, professional militaries of Jordan (under the renowned British anti-Semite, Glubb Pasha), Egypt, Syria, Iraq, and Lebanon. They had made a separated Israel into a still tiny but fully contiguous nation. This was proof that motivation is everything. If the Arabs lost, it would be a footnote in their histories. If the Jews lost, it would be a second Holocaust. The Jews did not lose.

Israel in June of 1967 had struck first against a gathering force of Arabs who had threatened to eliminate Israel and kill its inhabitants. The Arabs were well armed by the Soviet Union, who sought to dominate the Middle East by helping the Arabs, especially Egypt and Syria, smash Israel. This so-called Six-Day War had left Israel with the entire Sinai desert, the Golan Heights, a unified Jerusalem as part of Israel, and Israeli forces controlling the Gaza Strip. It had also left Israel with its forces on the eastern edge of the Suez Canal, thus able to keep it open or closed.

It was considered a military triumph without peer. The Israeli Air Force was now equipped by the United States with top-of-the-line Phantom F-4s and French Mirages. Its tanks were also equipped with high-end U.S.-made armor. Its soldiers were labeled as the best light infantry in the world.

Unfortunately, all of this led to serious overconfidence and carelessness by the Israelis, especially by Mrs. Golda Meir, prime minister of Israel. She had been a school teacher in Ohio before immigrating to Israel. She was a charming woman, but she had almost no military experience, and it showed.

She and the Israel Defense Forces (IDF) had allowed the fortifications on the east bank of the Suez Canal to deteriorate. The fortifications were manned by skeleton crews, if at all, on the first day of Yom Kippur, 1973, the most sacred day on the Jewish calendar, the Day of Atonement for one's sins of the prior year. The trenches and strongpoints in the Golan Heights had been insufficiently manned. In a word, Israel was unprepared.

Incredibly, this was despite warnings given to Israel by its own reconnaissance aircraft, by King Hussein of Jordan, and by Israel's number-one intelligence source in the Arab world, a Mr. Ashraf Marwan. He, almost unbelievably, was Anwar Sadat's son-in-law. He had warned Israel once before, and the warning turned out to be mistaken. Hence when he warned again just days before the commencement of the war, he was not believed.

The Egyptians, under what can only be called "genius"-level leadership by Sadat, had embarked upon a disinformation campaign to lull the Israelis into unpreparedness. Sadat had allowed large numbers of his soldiers to go on leave, had sent home twenty thousand Soviet military advisers, and had spoken warmly of his wish for peace. Israel's soldiers did not believe it, but Mrs. Meir and the major Israeli military hero, Moshe Dayan, did swallow the bait, hook, line, and sinker.

The Arabs knew that the time was ripe for an attack across the Suez Canal thanks to their own aerial observations and Russian satellite spying. They had made careful plans and prepared the right equipment for crossing the Suez Canal by silent rubber rafts. They had told the world that what they really wanted was their land back from the '67 war, but by negotiations, not by bloodshed.

Of course, this was a prevarication. They wanted "their" land back. Sadat had told his top generals he was willing to lose one million Egyptian lives to get it back. He meant it.

The Egyptians attacked in force early on October 6, 1973, and quickly overran most of the Israeli east bank of the Suez Canal fortifications, known as the Bar Lev Line. It had been considered impregnable.

At the same time, the Syrians, swimming in vast numbers of the best Soviet-made tanks, attacked in force at powerful positions manned inadequately in the Golan and quickly made progress, despite the incredible courage and skill of outnumbered Israeli tankers.

Mrs. Meir was called right away. The mighty Israeli Air Force was called into action right away. They were usually able to handle any kind of incursion by strafing and rocketing from the air. But this time was disastrously different.

Egypt and, to a lesser extent, Syria had been given the potent, brilliantly effective new SA-7 antiaircraft rocket in virtually unlimited quantities by the USSR. This weapon was so powerful that it could shoot down even the most skillfully piloted Israeli jets. Israel threw more and more aircraft at the advancing Egyptian Army as it approached a key line in the mountains of Sinai, the Mitla Pass. The results were terrible for the Israelis.

An unacceptable number of Israeli jets were being lost within hours and days.

Mrs. Meir was so discouraged that she had suicide pills out on her desk. Her ministers were telling her that Israel had the atom bomb and should use it on Egyptian and Syrian troop concentrations. Mrs. Meir did not want to hit the nuclear button.

Mrs. Meir had been misled by her landsman, Henry A. Kissinger. He had told Mrs. Meir that while he could clearly see from satellite photos that Egypt was mobilizing, she could not attack first, that if Israel "preempted" as they had in '67, world opinion would be so violently against them that Israel would "not get one nail" from the United States. Kissinger was sure that Israel could easily defeat any Arab force without striking first.

He told her that no matter what any data showed about Egyptian and Syrian concentrations, she must not strike first. To put it mildly, it was poor advice. Mrs. Meir and Israel were now paying the price.

She called Richard Nixon and told him how bad the situation was in the Sinai and on the Golan Heights. This was in the middle of the evening, Washington, DC, time. Richard Nixon said he would send help immediately. He immediately called the defense secretary, Mr. James Schlesinger, and ordered him to contact the Israeli minister of defense and find out what Israel needed.

The Israelis said they needed above all the "black boxes" that supremely good American scientists had created, working side by side with Israeli scientists. These devices could foil the SA-7, even though the SA-7 was a magnificently capable weapon. The United States had large stocks of these black boxes. Their workings were secret, but Israeli scientists had a general idea of how they worked.

Secretary Schlesinger, although a genuinely fine man, said he would not release the black boxes because their contents were so secret that he did not want them to possibly fall into Soviet hands.

Nixon told Mr. Schlesinger that he wanted the black boxes sent to Israel right away. The secretary of the U.S. Department of Defense (DOD) said it would take time because the black boxes had to be found in U.S. air bases, packed carefully, and then sent to Israel, which is five thousand miles away from Washington, DC.

Mr. Nixon spoke to Mrs. Meir again. She said Israel needed help immediately because the Egyptians and Syrians were breaking through Israeli lines and approaching Israeli cities.

Meanwhile, the U.S. leftist establishment was saying that the United States should not get involved at all. And Mr. Nixon was under nonstop attack in the leftist media over the Watergate "scandal." Nonstop. Vicious.

Then Mrs. Meir reiterated that Israel needed the black boxes. It was a matter of life and death. Mrs. Meir suggested that there undoubtedly were black boxes at the many U.S. bases in Europe close to Israel. Meanwhile, Mr. Nixon was visited by several Jewish friends of Israel at the White House, including my beloved father and Len Garment, who begged him to help Israel defend itself and the millions of Jewish men, women, and children whom the Egyptians and Syrians had promised to murder—to the cheers of adoring Arabs.

Mr. Nixon said he understood and would call Secretary Schlesinger again. The secretary said he would "work on it." Mr. Nixon said he did not want promises. He wanted the black boxes put on cargo planes immediately and sent off to Israel.

Mr. Schlesinger again said he would look into it. Purportedly, Nixon raised his voice and said he would call back in two hours and wanted to be certain that the devices were being flown to Israel.

Sure enough, roughly two hours later, Mr. Nixon called Secretary Schlesinger again and wanted to know if the devices were en route to Israeli air bases right at that moment.

The DOD boss said they were. Mr. Nixon called Mrs. Meir and said the black boxes were in the air. Supposedly, tears came to her eyes.

The Israelis were, then as now, geniuses at improvisation. As soon as the U.S. C-130s landed, with their freight of black boxes, the Israelis learned how to use them and attached them to their aircraft, and suddenly the SA-7s did not work any longer. The whole complexion of the war changed on a dime. In hours it was a revolution.

The Israeli airplanes, with their great pilots and great weaponry, stopped the Egyptian armor cold. The Egyptians were suddenly halted the way they had been in every other recent war. This was despite overwhelming numerical superiority in armor, artillery, and unusually fine leadership and strategy. In fact, the Egyptians fought quite differently from the way they had in other wars.

When faced with determined Israeli combat reserves and frontline discipline, the Egyptians had previously broken and run. This time they fought and did not withdraw. They counterattacked whenever possible. They were generations superior to the Egyptian forces of prior years, largely due to the inspirational leadership of Anwar Sadat. He was a genuine statesman, a rare quantity at any time and place. Whatever disparaging remarks were made about Arab soldiery in previous wars, by '73, they were first rate.

The same was true in the Golan Heights. The Syrians had started the attack with a roughly eight-to-one advantage in tanks—and they were extremely good Soviet-made T-60s, which were direct scions of the famous T-34 tank that had played such an immense part in beating the führer in World War II. The Syrians had a good plan of attack and had real prospects of breaking through the thin Israeli lines and invading en masse into central Israel, where there were no clear lines of defense. The Syrian armor had been protected from the Israelis' air force by the SA-7.

Then came the black boxes, and suddenly their antiaircraft rockets didn't work quite as well, and the burning hulks of Syrian Soviet-made tanks littered the otherwise inspiring landscape on whose peaks were studded with Soviet-made pillboxes built for the Syrians and lost in the mad rush of Israeli success in the Six-Day War of 1967.

The Syrians responded by sending in large masses of previously uncommitted armor. The Israelis sent in their tanks, fabulously well motivated and led. These largely were upgraded and modernized versions of the British Centurion.

The result was the second-largest tank battle of all time, behind the Nazi-Soviet Battle of Kursk in 1943.

Incredibly, in the Battle of Kursk, although the war had been going on for two years adversely to Hitler, he was able to assemble almost thirteen hundred first-rate tanks to attempt to pinch off a large Soviet bulge near Kursk in Ukraine. The Soviets, masters of the situation, had assembled more than thirty-two hundred tanks, including the T-34. The Soviets had been briefed thoroughly on Hitler's plans and even knew the exact date and time of the proposed Nazi offensive thanks to

British intelligence. They had dug extensive antitank ditches. Their artillery advantage was breathtaking.

Nevertheless, on July 3, 1943, the führer ordered the onset of Operation Citadel, the Kursk offensive. It was a disaster for the Nazis. But it did make history as the largest armor battle ever.

In the Israeli-Syrian tank battle of the Golan Heights in 1973, the number of tanks involved on both sides well exceeded three thousand. The Syrians had a roughly eight-to-one advantage in tanks, but the Israeli tankers were well trained—and most of all, well motivated. (It is amazing that Israel was able to assemble such a large force of tanks when one notes that Israel had a population of fewer than six million compared with Hitler's close to ninety million.)

At the dawn of battle on October 6, 1973, the Syrians made inroads under the SA-7 umbrella. Their usual losses due to Israeli air power were greatly reduced, and they advanced rapidly. But once that was halted by the evening of October 9, largely although not entirely due to the black boxes, the lines had stabilized. The Syrians, also greatly improved from '67, repeatedly attempted to resume the offensive and at times did so brilliantly.

(One of the biggest myths of the Middle East ongoing crisis is that the Arabs are not good fighters. Some of them are not great, but others are amazingly brave.)

But Israel stopped these assaults and pushed eastward, making an immense bulge in the Syrian lines and approaching the capital of Damascus.

Within about six days of the beginning of the Egyptian/Syrian invasion, the possibility of Israel encircling and cutting off Cairo and Damascus looked real. This would have been a humiliation for the Arab side as well as for the Soviets. The Soviets stepped in and announced that if Israel did not back off and retreat to the lines where the conflict started, it would land Soviet paratroopers in front of the Israeli lines.

These soldiers would at the least enforce a cease-fire so that Israeli forces could not take Cairo and/or Damascus.

The problems only grew from there. The Soviets would be left with a large land army in the Middle East. At the time, this was a desperately important place on the globe for its oil production as well as for its significance to a worldwide population of well over one billion Muslims.

The United States would be frozen out of that hot, sandy spot on the globe just as our oil and gas output fell drastically relative to our consumption.

The president was under nonstop political attack over Watergate and anything else the opposition in Congress, the universities, and the media could think of. Much but by no means all of the opposition leaders and spokesmen were Jewish.

The burdens that Mr. Nixon carried were almost unbelievable. Compounding these were threats by OPEC, the Organization of Petroleum Exporting Countries, most of which were majority Muslim, to stop shipping oil to the United States if the United States continued to send arms to Israel. This would exacerbate an already difficult inflation and growth picture for the United States.

The "sensible" step for Mr. Nixon at that point would have been to back off support for Israel and to agree to a multinational push for a cease-fire and then an Israeli withdrawal.

That would have left Syria free to attack and invade Israel through the Golan Heights again. It would have left Egypt in possession of both sides of the Suez Canal and a good foothold in the Sinai. Israel would have been in the most precarious position it had been in since before the Six-Day War. There were a great many in Congress, the media, and the universities who thought it was Israel's duty as a Jewish, civilized state to offer its jugular to the killer's knife. That would have been the "sensible" thing to do.

Mr. Nixon did not take the "sensible" step though. Instead of being pushed around by the UN, the Arabs, and the Soviet Union, he stood up for Israel and for the United States.

He told the Soviets his feelings about their aggressive posture by ordering U.S. forces around the world to go to DEFCON 2, which was shorthand for Defense Condition 2. It is the last step before nuclear war. That is, Richard M. Nixon, who had been called the worst kind of anti-Semite and Nazi, risked nuclear war to back Israel.

This was an unprecedented stand for the Jewish people by a world leader.

Nothing like it had ever happened before in the six-thousand-year-old history of the Jews. It was unheard of. It was by no means an easily unanimous decision within the administration. There was backbiting and backstabbing within the Nixon White House.

Of course, in the media, he was called a gambler with the world's future, and in a way, he was.

But no more so than John F. Kennedy was in the Cuban Missile Crisis of 1962. Of course, JFK was hailed as a hero. Nixon was reviled and cursed at by the media and the beautiful people.

The Soviets at that point in the world's history were run largely by a committee of the politburo. Committees rarely take immense risks. Neither did the Soviets. They sent their top foreign policy people to meet with Nixon and Kissinger and quickly dropped their threat to use their elite paratroops in the Middle East.

In short order, the Israelis, who had been seriously frightened by events—to the point that Mrs. Meir (again) reportedly had suicide pills out on her desk—agreed to talks with the Arabs.

Then the official Palestinian savior committee, the United Nations, stepped in, as usual.

Now, please bear this in mind—Israel is officially the Jewish state. It had been born out of the pitiful remnants of European Jewry surviving after the Holocaust plus the few thousand Jews who had managed to stay there during the two hundred years or more of Turkish rule and then a few decades of a British Mandate from the League of Nations after World War II.

The surrounding Arabs had tried to kill it and massacre the Jews there since its founding in 1948. Israel, against fearful odds, had withstood all attacks on its people.

Israel had almost no friends on this earth. At one time, when France was fighting the Arab rebellion in Algeria, it sent weapons to Israel as a fellow combatant against Arabs. That stopped in the late 1960s as Algeria became an independent state and immense numbers of Israel-hating, Jew-hating Arabs moved to metropolitan France. This made France stop helping Israel in any way.

The British had sold Israel weapons in the 1960s, but soon the left-wing, Israel-hating Laborite Party made Britain stop doing such sales.

Israel's only friend was the United States. In the UN, there were hundreds of resolutions passed year after year condemning

Israel for everything imaginable. There were over a hundred anti-Israel states in the UN endlessly voting to condemn and punish Israel. The resolutions gushed out of the United Nations printing press. Every time, these were vetoed by the United States.

But the United States had never been a big supplier of weapons of defense to Israel. Harry Truman had voted to create Israel. But he supplied no weapons to Israel at all. He went along with laws severely punishing Americans who helped Israel with arms and fighters. Lyndon Johnson had done nothing at all to help Israel when the Jewish state stood surrounded by the Egyptians, Syrian, Jordanians, Iraqis, and Saudis before the Six-Day War. He did not lift a finger, although he did again veto wildly anti-Israel motions in the UN.

John F. Kennedy was a handsome man and had many Jewish friends, admirers, and biographers. He sold almost nothing to Israel in the way of arms, although JFK, like all American presidents, signed legislation authorizing U.S. civil aid to Israel.

One U.S. president had stood up and said that no matter what world opinion said, no matter what the anti-Semites in Congress said (and there were plenty, headed by William Fulbright, Democrat of Arkansas, but there were enemies of Israel in the GOP as well), no matter what the media powerhouses said against Israel, led by the Jewish-owned *New York Times*, he would do what he believed was right: He would save Israel. He would save the children of Israel, in the Promised Land.

That man was Richard M. Nixon, whom the media had falsely labeled as a racist anti-Semite. I was extremely proud to work for him. I rarely saw Mr. Nixon at that stage of my life and his. I did not start full time at the White House until after the cease-fire went into effect. Even after I did start, when I saw Mr. Nixon, it was on those extremely infrequent occasions when he called me in to discuss a message I had written over his name to Congress discussing some immensely important subject such as energy or insurance.

These meetings—again, infrequent—were always in his hideaway office in the EOB. Mr. Nixon looked steadily more exhausted day by day. Now, bear in mind, he had already rescued Israel while he was under the harshest political pressure and the vilest personal attacks I could imagine. It showed on his face. Yet he had done his greatest duty as he (and I) saw it. I was deeply touched to be in his presence.

Again, I stress that while I had the great pleasure and honor of spending "personal time" with Mr. Nixon after he left office, I rarely saw him when I was working at the WH. But when I did, I endlessly thought that I was in the presence, working hand in glove, of the man who had saved the children of Israel, a genuinely Old Testament presence.

I had been hired on at the White House largely because I was both a lawyer and an economist. Mr. Nixon could use all the help he could get in both areas.

As soon as I started, there was plenty of work to be done that involved economics. There was the terrible Arab oil embargo after the Yom Kippur War, and the inflation and recession it dragged in its wake. There was at the same time a growing hue and cry about air and water pollution.

Mr. Nixon, no stranger to difficulties and challenges, threw himself into the challenge. He convened a committee of cabinet members; the deputy head of the Office of Management and Budget, a math whiz named Paul O'Neill; and some solons to create an answer.

That answer was the first energy independence bill. It would combine "clean energy" efforts on a massive scale with greatly increased research into new sources of energy, such as the use of the virtually limitless power of ocean currents and waves.

The project was called (at my humble suggestion) Project Independence.

On one meeting with RN, when I was sitting with my yellow legal pad in my hands and several BIC ballpoint pens in my shirt pocket, I noticed to my embarrassment that one of the pens had apparently leaked ink onto my pink Oxford cloth Brooks Brothers shirt.

Mr. Nixon studied the energy message in front of me. And then he asked me how wave power worked. I tried to explain to him that, as I understood it, it was akin to a large hydroelectric source of power striking a windmill of immense size and turning generators but with no end point. It was an endless source of power that created no pollution at all except for the massive amounts of sand and concrete that went into making it. Beyond that, scientists knew about it, I said, but few if anyone else.

"But you personally, the graduate of Yale Law School with the genius father, don't know exactly?" he asked me.

"I wish I did," I said, "and thank you for your kind words. We can call Paul O'Neill. He'll know. He knows everything."

Mr. N looked at me with a smile. "I don't know either. And if anyone in Congress sends back a detailed question about how waves off Maine can power a lightbulb in Southern California, we can refer him to Paul O'Neill, and then he can refer the congressman or senator to someone he knows, and everyone will work at blinding speed to produce an answer that no one will ever understand.

"The couple of sentences you just gave me are the closest anyone is ever going to get to an answer that the voters will understand."

"I'll make sure Paul sends you and me a memo about it right away," I said earnestly. "And thank you once again for your kind words."

Mr. Nixon waved the thought away. "No," he said. "No one on Capitol Hill is going to even understand enough about it to ask a question."

Then he paused, got up, and picked up a sturdy gray elephant sculpture from a shelf. "The thing you have to understand, Ben," he said with mock solemnity, "is that your average representative to Congress is not fit to be a dog catcher."

I laughed out loud, and Mr. Nixon, who liked a good audience response, followed up: "There are very few on Capitol Hill who are geniuses like your father—and you too, from what Julie tells me."

"Sir, I am humbled," I said, or words to that effect. "But there were people at Yale who were much smarter than I was, and my father always told me that there were people at Williams College who were smarter than he was."

Mr. Nixon waved my comment away with a serious look as if he were concentrating. "Modesty. That's what people say about your father too." He went on. "The real question is about that ballpoint pen leak on your shirt. It's amazing that the BIC corporation, which I think is French and probably has made literally billions, maybe trillions, of those pens, still cannot make them so that occasionally one does not leak."

"I agree."

"But if they screw up, even if it's in no way your fault, it makes you look bad."

"Very true," I said. "It won't happen again."

"Really? But how can you possibly know if it will happen again?" he asked. "But it's fascinating," he said as he looked at me with sincere attention. "This is the way it happens to you with your shirt, and this is what happens to me with Watergate. Some idiot screws up with some imbecilic plan to bug the DNC headquarters. I have no idea whose idea it was originally, and I still don't know. And I have no idea what they were looking for there. None at all. And I don't think Bob Haldeman knows, and for sure Ehrlichman doesn't know.

"And we all get blamed for it as if we cooked it up here at the White House. And we didn't. I didn't know a thing about it until Bob Haldeman came in here with a newspaper clipping about it. Not a word.

"But because I helped expose Alger Hiss about twenty-five years ago, the press still hates me and thinks if anything even questionable happened, it has to be my fault and my purpose. Yes. It's just as much nonsense as if I made that pen that leaked onto your shirt.

"And by the way, that's a fine Oxford cloth Brooks Brothers shirt."

"Thank you," I said. I was always impressed at how carefully RN noticed everything that was going on around him.

"How old are you, Ben?"

"Twenty-eight."

"Ben, I couldn't have afforded that shirt or anything from Brooks Brothers at twenty-eight. It wasn't a hardship. I wasn't in the fashion game anyway. It wasn't until I was in law practice in

New York City that I could afford pretty much anything I wanted to wear. That's a good feeling. It didn't mean a lot to me, but I think it meant a lot to Pat, and I felt bad about it for a long time."

"I understand. I've never had that feeling, but I have an idea about it."

"We have some people here at the EOB who can buy and sell me a million times over. Your pal Peter Flanigan. Your friend Roy Ash. Lots of others. And Pat had to do with a 'good Republican cloth coat.'"

(How did he know Peter and I were pals? Peter's great-grandparents had founded Anheuser-Busch. Peter's father had put together Manufacturers Hanover Trust. He was stupendously smart. He had been a naval carrier fighter pilot during World War II in the Pacific. He was as handsome as a movie star could be. Mr. Nixon had been friends with the Flanigans more or less forever.)

(How did he know that Roy and I were close friends? Roy Ash had come from modest beginnings to graduate at the top of his class at Harvard Business School. His ambition had been to be a branch manager of a Bank of America unit. Instead, he and his business school classmate, "Tex" Thornton, founded one of the first supersuccessful conglomerates: Litton Industries. He greatly compounded that by buying a sheep and cattle ranch in Nevada as a tax shelter. He later added a few hundred acres of scrub to "even up the property lines" to simplify tax shelter boundaries. He bought them from a grizzled old prospector who insisted there was a rich vein of gold there until his dying breath.)

(Those few hundred acres turned out to be the richest, most valuable lode of gold in the Lower 48 ever found, making Roy Ash one of the richest men on earth.)

(Finally, as to RN and what he knew about his staff, how did he have any idea that I would get that reference to the "good Republican cloth coat" from the 1952 Checkers speech? I was only seven at the time of that highly effective speech. He knew almost too much.)

(In that same connection, I observed many closed doors at the EOB with names that told me nothing about who they were or what they did. Could Mr. Nixon know in detail who each of these people was and what he or she did? What was going on? I never learned why Mr. Nixon felt so comfortable musing with me. Was it because I had written so much about him in op-eds already? Or because he knew my father and mother? I never learned his motivations. I did observe a Sherlock Holmes level of care, almost as if he were a detective investigating his own life. This same scale of scanning what was going on around him reached moral issues as well—although not consistently.)

As time passed at the White House, Dave Gergen, my direct boss, occasionally asked me to do something really difficult. The most difficult of all had to do with Mr. and Mrs. Nixon's taxes. It came about one night when I was working late, as I almost always did, on an endless project about universal health care.

This was a very rare case because it involved taxes, health, morals, and votes all at once. It was (as I recall) the only time, or one of the only times, that Mr. Nixon actually stuck his head into my office, which was rare indeed.

Ray Price and Mr. Nixon and two sturdy-looking men in blue coveralls appeared at my door. The men in coveralls were pulling a trolley on which were two good-sized cardboard boxes, and on them were the initials "RN" and "PN." There might have been other men in suits, Secret Service men, in the hall outside. I don't recall.

With a big smile on his always cheerful face, Ray said that he had a project for me. "Which only you can do, young Professor Stein," the president of the United States said to me with an ironic smile.

Then with a deeply furrowed brow, Ray Price gestured at the boxes, and with an added theatrical measure, he waved at the workmen and bowed to them and to the boxes.

"The problem—" said Ray, and here Mr. Nixon interrupted: "As if we didn't have enough problems." We all laughed, except for the workmen, who had apparently not been let in on the joke. "—is this," Mr. Price went on. "A question has arisen about Mr. Nixon's taxes."

"The question is whether I can take a deduction for donating to the National Archives our personal papers for the past four years," Mr. Nixon said. "There is plenty of precedent for taking the deduction, but LBJ took such a huge deduction that the law was tightened up quite a lot in 1969, and the government now takes the position that the papers always belonged to them and no one else. Therefore, I can't take a deduction for a donation to the National Archives because the papers already belonged to the National Archives."

I nodded as if I understood what they were talking about.

"The rumor around here is that you did extremely well on tax at Yale. Thus, you must know what the law is. And if you don't know the score, you can always ask your father, and he'll know," added Ray Price. "The problem is that we don't want you to discuss any of this with anyone but us. Not even with Dave Gergen. Not even your father."

"We'd like for you to read these papers and figure out a way we can legitimately take a deduction of about $4 million against my 1969 taxes," said Mr. Nixon.

"And it all has to be totally legitimate," Mr. Nixon added. "Cannot even be questioned."

He gave me a smile that said (to me, at least) that he recognized that the line had been lifted from some byplay between Peter Lorre and Humphrey Bogart in *Casablanca*. That was the first and only time I had seen or heard of him taking anything from a movie. I might have been wrong thinking it was taken from *Casablanca*. Maybe it was Mr. Nixon's original way of expressing himself.

I took a long gulp and said, "I assume there is no case law on this subject. That is, there is no case 'on all fours' with your situation, where a court has said that a public official cannot take a deduction for papers created when he was a civil servant on the public payroll."

Mr. Nixon shrugged and turned up his hands in an "I don't know" gesture.

Ray Price looked at me and said, "That's why we came to you. We didn't go to the valedictorian of the Harvard Law School class of 1970."

"Yes, but you give me way too much credit," I replied, inwardly astounded that Mr. Nixon and Ray Price knew so much about me. "I was basically elected by my classmates because I was the most well liked. Not because I was the best at legal research."

(And well liked, I might have added, largely because of my wild and crazy anti–Vietnam War classroom theatrics.)

At that point, Ray Price took a piece of scratch paper and wrote down a man's name and phone number in New York

City. There was no internet or email then. "Do all you can, and if you can't come up with an answer by morning, please call this man. He's the best tax lawyer in New York, as far as we know." Then he handed me the sheet of paper.

Mr. Nixon looked at me with his sympathetic brown eyes and shook my hand. "Good luck, Counselor," he said. Then he and Ray Price walked out the door.

I immediately took the lids off the boxes and started sifting through the stacks of papers inside. They were all 1040 forms for Richard M. Nixon and Patricia Ryan Nixon, with many supporting documents. There were also a few law review articles and some appellate court opinions on the subject in question.

It was about midnight when I started reading and about six in the morning when I lay down on my satin couch, absolutely exhausted and temporarily defeated.

As I read it, there was simply no question at all that the papers were created on government property, on government time, with government support, such as researchers and secretaries. The articles that Mr. Price and Mr. Nixon supplied to me were unequivocally clear law review pieces that showed that appellate courts had absolutely no problem at all denying requests for tax deductions for gifts such as Mr. Nixon's.

To my great regret, because I was a huge fan of Mr. Nixon, it was crystal clear that Mr. Nixon was not going to get that deduction.

However, I was only three years out of law school. There might be case law that I did not know about.

I went home to sleep at my tiny little rented house in Georgetown with my faithful dog, Mary, by my side. At about ten in the morning, I awoke and called the lawyer in New York who had apparently drawn up the tax return that was being questioned by the IRS. The man answered the call immediately.

I laid out the case as I saw it, and the gentleman lawyer cleared his throat and said, "Well, Ben, I can tell you one big thing that occurs to me: I'm damned glad that it's you who's handling this case and not me. I don't know how on earth you get out of this with the deduction."

"Sir," I said to the esteemed lawyer on the other end of the line, "didn't you draw up this tax return?"

My recollection is that he did not answer except with a variation on "You can't blame a guy for trying."

At that point, I was literally sick to my stomach. How had the president gotten into such a mess? Such a clear-cut, no-bones-about-it mess? I lay down in bed with Mary, and then the phone started ringing and didn't stop.

I finally answered. It was Dave Gergen, my boss, the nicest of the nice guys. "Why aren't you in your office?" he asked.

"I have a badly upset stomach," I said.

"You have to get into the office right away," he said sternly.

"I can't. I don't feel well enough to drive."

"We'll send a car for you," he said.

"I don't feel well," I said.

Dave paused for a moment. "Look," he said, "you have to be here. If you don't come in here right now, you're going to get called before the grand jury."

By the "grand jury," he could only have meant the Watergate grand jury, which the hanging judge, the Roy Bean of DC, Judge John Sirica, also called "Maximum John" for his harsh sentences, had empaneled to hear every scrap of craziness about RN.

"Why?" I asked. "I haven't had a thing to do with Watergate. You know that very well."

"Just get in here right away," he said. "I'll send a car."

Sure enough, in about fifteen minutes, there was a shiny black White House car in front of my tiny house in Georgetown. I had gotten dressed. Dosed myself thoroughly with Lomotil. And soon I was on my way to the EOB. I staggered down the hall to Dave's office. He asked me what I had been doing. I told him I was not allowed to discuss it.

"All right," he said. "Was it about the president's taxes?"

"I just told you: I was told by Ray Price not to discuss it."

"So it's not about Watergate?"

"Dave, as far as I'm concerned, there is no Watergate. It's all a fraud and a delusion."

"That's great," he answered. "That's perfect. All right. You can go home now."

"I will need that car. I didn't drive," I told him. "Anyway, I'm going to go to my office and work for a little while, and then my friend will drive me home."

This issue I was dealing with was *not* what Dave was asking about. Milton Curtiss Rose, the lawyer in New York, wrote a brief and answered the IRS's questions, and we all prayed.

I wrote a small piece of the brief, about how much of RN's work was done all by himself, seated on an easy chair, writing on a yellow legal pad. Surely those were by far the most valuable parts of the Nixon papers. Surely they were not covered by the general rule about work products done by civil servants.

It didn't matter. The judge said that Mr. Nixon could not—repeat, *not*—take that deduction. At that point, to my shock, the White House operator called me and said that the president was on the line. "Ben," Mr. Nixon said, "you did a nice job on that part of the brief. I think we could take it up on appeal after appeal and eventually win."

"It will take years," I replied. "But, Mr. President, this is how the Communist Party won all their court victories in the 1950s. They just kept appealing and appealing and appealing until they found a judge who liked them."

"But we're different. I'm in the cross hairs all the time. Every single time my lawyers appear before a court, the media will use it as an excuse to say that 'Nixon didn't pay his taxes.'"

"Yes, sir," I said.

"So then I get shot at more or less constantly. Endlessly. And what if I don't find a court that doesn't like me?"

"Yes, sir," I agreed. "A likely possibility too."

"So your argument is quite correct about the easy chair in Key Biscayne and the yellow legal pads. I wish I had you on my legal staff. But just because an argument is good doesn't mean a court will like it. It all depends on the attitude and outlook of the judge."

"Sir, this is just exactly the 'legal realism' that Professor Bork taught us in law school. That was developed and nurtured at Yale."

"I know," said that smart president. "People think I'm stupid. But I know one or two things."

Then he hung up. The tax issue went to the federal court of appeals for the DC Circuit. We were shot down, and Mr. Nixon decided not to take up the matter any further, as I recall. In any event, he paid the tax. It has always seemed to me that he was badly mistreated, but then it's not at all rare for taxpayers to be mistreated by tax collectors. There is something about that in the Bible. And it was certainly not at all unusual for Richard Nixon to be mistreated.

CHAPTER SEVEN

LAWYER, POLITICIAN, PERFORMER

Something about the incident had made at least a small impression on Mr. Nixon about me.

From then on, occasionally, rarely, I was invited to cabinet meetings. I would sit in a chair on the edge of the room. I was not expected to speak at the meetings, and I didn't. Most Americans do not get to attend cabinet meetings, and I thought I was blessed indeed to see this major phenomenon of American democracy at work.

Several things emerged from those meetings to take a lodgment in my memories.

First of all, Mr. Nixon had a superb sense of humor. At one point in the larger world, statistics started to indicate, sadly, that we might be heading for a bout of inflation, even as we were also heading into an economic slowdown. This was a major political problem, to put it mildly.

"We'll have to appoint a commission to study the whole issue," Mr. Nixon said. "That will solve the problem."

"I assume you are kidding," said someone whose name I do not recall. "We all know that those commissions accomplish nothing at all. It's just a way of avoiding questions for a few weeks."

"I know that," Mr. Nixon said. "I've been in this game for a while now."

"But can you tell people you expect any concrete results?" asked the same man.

"Of course we can," Mr. Nixon said. "Honesty may not be the best policy, but it's worth trying once in a while."

There was laughter in the room, and Mr. Nixon, who liked being liked, smiled.

Another participant in the room suggested that we might have a wage-price freeze as we did in 1971, with extremely good short-term results. (My father was in charge of phase one of this event. In its initial phases, we got no inflation to speak of, a jump in employment, and a rise in corporate results. My father was on network TV saying that on that day, about a month into phase one, the statistics on the economy were the best they had been ever. The stats fell considerably after that. Economists teach that wage-price controls rarely work out well, and they are right. Now no one even remotely remembers phase one except for me, and that's because I have a huge trove of photographs of the participants in the meeting at Camp David, where the wage-price freeze was agreed upon. As it happens, even as I was revising the first draft of this book, Jeffrey E. Garten— a fine writer from Yale—released a book on this subject called *Three Days at Camp David*. I recommend it heartily.)

Mr. Nixon looked beguiled and intrigued at a suggestion about reissuing guidelines that had been so controversial. This prompted another man in the room to say, "Mr. President, you can't walk on water twice."

The president looked serious and replied, "You can if it's frozen."

More laughter. The president liked that too.

From that I realized that Mr. Nixon was a lawyer and a politician, but he was also a performer. He loved performing, and he did it well.

Another event of that time that stands out in my memory is that by a miracle, I became closer friends with Julie and David Eisenhower. I am not sure how it started, but probably it had a lot to do with my affection for King Timahoe, Pasha, and Vicki. I was occasionally called by the assistant to some other assistant and asked if I wanted to walk the dogs. I always did. It was a thrill to get up from my typewriter and have the dogs meet me in West Executive Avenue and then take their leashes and walk them around the back lawn of the White House.

I really could not believe my luck that this was a part of my life.

It got better because my father often joined me and the dogs on these walks. For some reason, perhaps "euphoric recall," my recollection is that the weather was always good on these walks. My father and I talked about the grim tidings of Watergate and how unlikely it was that Mr. Nixon would finish his term. Now when I think about it, I simply cannot believe that Mr. Nixon was made to leave office over a "crime" he did not commit.

If only there had been an internet or Fox News or Newsmax.

Anyway, I was extremely happy at the White House. Dave Gergen never mentioned anything about a grand jury again. He had a superb sense of humor. Perhaps he was just playing a game.

On one occasion, I was invited by Julie and David Eisenhower to have lunch with them at the White House Solarium.

This was a room much resembling a small greenhouse. I had never known it existed. At first we were all cheerful, but then the mood became extremely serious. I think that both Julie and David knew that a media coup was unfolding and that there was not a lot that could be done about it.

Nevertheless, I felt as if I were on Mount Olympus with the gods. That was partly because of the setting. But mostly it was because of my hosts.

Julie Eisenhower is the finest woman I have ever known except for my wife. *Saint* is not too strong a word for her. While the world was collapsing around her because of a marauding leftist and nihilist media and its cohorts in politics, she was polite, modest, and self-effacing. She is also amazingly beautiful. I have rarely broken bread with any woman as stunningly beautiful as she is.

And supersmart. Obviously, I knew her father was a genius, but I realized that her mother was also extremely smart and well educated. She did what every well-mannered person is supposed to do—ask questions of his or her companions and not just talk about themselves—but extremely few do.

David was also deeply impressive. Here he is, I thought, the grandson of the supreme Allied commander Europe and one of the most well-loved presidents of all time. He was himself a graduate of a major prestige school, Amherst College, one of the finest small colleges in the nation. He was also a former naval officer; a lawyer with a degree from George Washington University Law School, the same school my wife attended before her meteoric career as a lawyer; and also a teacher of history at a fine university. But he was as self-effacing as a person can be.

You could not possibly have made even a rough guess at his pedigree upon sitting with him.

It occurred to me over and over that I was dining with people whose ancestors were presidents and superstar generals but might as well have been the children of local high school principals.

Of course, it was already crystal clear to me that Richard Nixon was a great man. A biblical hero. But he also had to have been the best possible father. And Pat Nixon had to have been the best possible mother.

I have been in touch with them closely since then, and my opinions of them have gone nowhere but up.

CHAPTER EIGHT

GUILTY FIRST, TRIAL SECOND:
IT MATTERS A LOT WHO YOUR LAWYER IS

At a certain point in the saga of the phony Watergate "scandal," the Democrat-controlled Congress created at least one (and maybe more than one) special Watergate Committee. The idea was to impeach and convict Richard Nixon of certain crimes (all fictitious) that supposedly happened in connection with the break-in at the Watergate Hotel in June 1972. No one has ever specified what the burglars were looking for at the DNC HQ at the Watergate, nor has anyone ever shown that RN had any guilty knowledge of anything connected with Watergate.

That did not matter to the Watergate lynch mob attacking RN and trying to reverse the greatest electoral vote landscape of all American history. "Guilty first, trial second," as the children's fairy tale goes.

The Watergate Committee drew up about twelve articles of impeachment against Mr. Nixon. One of them had to do with the 1972 GOP Nominating Convention at a Sheraton Hotel in or near San Diego. The allegation—hazy, to be sure—was that the parent company of Sheraton, an early conglomerate called ITT, had paid a large bribe to the GOP, and in return, the GOP would publicize the hotel and also would make the Justice Department drop some antitrust cases against ITT.

Because I was and am both a lawyer and an economist with some training in antitrust, I was ordered to work on the ITT/Sheraton matter.

As is usual in such cases, I was given a stack of documents to read and then a list of people in high places in government who might know about the matter.

It took only a short time to figure out something that should have been obvious to anyone of even medium experience about the ITT/Sheraton matter. The timeline did not work out for there to have been a bribe. There was much too much of a time spread between the selection of the GOP convention venue and the conversations about the antitrust matter. Plus, the persons in charge of both matters were far apart in age and location, and some were not living at the time they supposedly made key decisions and orders.

It was as if (in a greatly simplified way) Julius Caesar were accused of murdering Robert Kennedy. Or as if the South Carolinians had fired on Fort Sumter and thus had caused the Napoleonic Wars or the War of the Revolution. The timeline just did not make sense.

This was a fascinating project. I had to call many high-ranking people involved in making decisions of this kind. Cabinet members. High officials of the GOP. Top dogs at the Office of Management and Budget. Even people at ITT and Sheraton. One in particular, who became a fantastically successful entrepreneur, took my call while he was at a handball game at a local club. Breathless and earnest, he answered my questions in great detail.

I submitted my findings to my superiors. They transmitted them to the legal team that was working on defending President Nixon. In turn, they were transmitted to the Watergate Committee of Congress.

In very short order, we got a notice that this particular item was being dropped from the list of "offenses" for which Mr. Nixon was being impeached. As I later learned, this was the only item dropped from that list.

Very soon, the White House operator was on the phone with me with a call from Mr. Nixon.

In a hearty, cheery voice, he told me he was happy about the result. "You did a fine job on that, Ben," he said. "I wish the rest of my lawyers were as adroit as you or playing on their feet as well as you."

"Sir," I said, "I cannot tell you what a pleasure and an honor it is to be working on behalf of you and your presidency" (or words to that effect).

He thanked me and asked me if I would have a few words with his actual "legal team." This was a group of young lawyers sent over from the bureaucracy "on loan" to the White House for the crisis. I spent a couple of hours with them later that day. I told them what I believed to be true: there simply was no evidence of any real crime. Mr. Nixon's only "crime" as far as I could tell was that the beautiful people in the media hated him.

They had always hated him. His spectacular win in the 1972 election was simply more reason to hate him. "Just assume that everything in the indictments [or whatever they were called then] is simply a group of fraternity boys gossiping about a guy they hated because he always won elections for class office," I told them.

It's been a long time. I do not recall what the legal team said to me in response. I just recall thinking, as I left their offices, that I had rarely been among a less impressive bunch of lawyers.

I called some of my higher-ups and reported my assessment of the situation. As far as I know, nothing was ever done to correct the situation. To this day, roughly fifty years down the road, I am still mystified that the president of the United States, in a matter of political life and death, had such poor representation.

I called Julie and pleaded with her to consider using a brilliant member of my class at Yale, Bill Jeffress, a real genius, to head Mr. Nixon's defense team. Interestingly enough, Mr. Nixon did not take up that suggestion but later used some of my suggestions for legal defense in litigation over the possession of his papers. He got predictably good results. It matters a lot who your lawyer is.

Just a few days after that, as I was walking down the hallway of the Executive Office Building to see my boss, the redoubtable Dave Gergen, I ran into Mr. Nixon with a small detail of men, presumably Secret Service or Executive Protective Service or whatever they were called at that time.

He gave me a big smile and stuck out his hand to shake mine, just as he had recently held out his hand to greet Chinese premier Chou En-lai (Zhou Enlai). He shook my hand warmly.

"You did a great job on that nonsense about ITT and Sheraton, Ben," he said. "Your father would be proud."

"Thank you, sir," I said.

"It was like an episode of Perry Mason," he said. "You just connected the dots and came out with the answer."

"Thank you, again, Mr. President," I said. "I really feel as if it's the high point of my life to have been able to help you in any way at all. After all, you saved Israel. I would do anything for you."

The president laughed and said, "Don't let the Watergate Committee hear you. You'll be in front of the grand jury in no time at all."

I smiled humbly, and Mr. Nixon said, "Someday we'll talk about Israel and the American Jews."

Then he walked on. Even now, and it's been a long, long time, my head spins when I think about it.

Again, decades have passed. I was a young man then, and I am an old man now. Friends often ask me what it was like to work for Mr. Nixon at the White House during Watergate. The phrase that comes to mind is usually a quote from Talleyrand: "He who has not lived before the Revolution does not know the sweetness of life and cannot imagine that there can be happiness in life." (This is not the precise quote.)

Life in the EOB was glorious. We knew that we were beleaguered. Most of us on the speech-writing staff knew that Mr. Nixon's days as president were numbered.

But we were almost always in a cheerful mood. The analogy that occurs to me is that in 1954, the French Army was besieged inside its fortifications in an area known as Dien Bien Phu in what became North Vietnam (now just Vietnam). The Communists and their friends from China and the USSR had the fortress completely surrounded. The area around it was a dense jungle. It was impossible for the French, with an obsolete and decaying air force, to adequately resupply Dien Bien Phu with food or medicine or ammunition. The French soldiers were doomed to death or capture by the enemy.

Yet even then, the French were deluged with volunteers from the French Army and the French Foreign Legion wanting to be air-dropped into the enclave to fight to the end. (One of the biggest lies of the past hundred years is that the French were bad soldiers. They never were. They were powerful warriors and poorly led, and their heroics in and around Dunkirk basically saved Great Britain from the Nazis.)

Similarly, even with the end approaching for the RN presidency, there was considerable enthusiasm for RN in the White House. The mood was superb. I have worked at many jobs since the days of RN: as a university teacher; a columnist for the *Wall Street Journal*; a scriptwriter; a novelist; an investigator into financial fraud for *Barron's* and in litigation; a columnist for the late, greatly lamented *Los Angeles Herald Examiner*; a writer and commentator on economics; an actor; a game show host; a talk show host; and a father and husband.

In no other venue was morale as high as it was in the Nixon White House, at least among us speechwriters and our magnificent research staff. Our staff meetings were filled with good humor and bantering and group support. Dave Gergen, our direct boss, was an excellent leader. Every one of us except one who shall be nameless was wholeheartedly devoted to RN and believed in him. Of the WH speech-writing and research staff, all put in their best efforts until the very last.

I was among the most devoted, mostly because of RN's salvation of Israel and also because of my father's connection with RN and my mother's fanatical attachment to him. But Ken Khachigian, who became a major political adviser to conservatives in sunny California and a supersuccessful lawyer, was as devoted. Aram Bakshian was as devout as yours truly and far smarter.

The amazing fact that I was working at the most interesting place on the earth at that time, within a short walk to my father and an even shorter walk to my girlfriend, Pat, a researcher for the CEA, was also magnificent. (I was by this time divorced from my first wife. We remarried in 1977, and she is my heart's blood. She was not always pro-RN, as noted, but at this point, she would cheerfully commit murder for RN. Pat has not spoken to me since 1976. God bless her.)

I had the incredible privilege of working on a staff that had some of the very smartest, most well-educated men and women on the planet. I worked with some amazingly smart lawyers at the Federal Trade Commission, and two of them are still close friends. But the two men who worked on either side of me in the EOB were not only superbrilliant but also poetic, followers of history and the arts, and genuine Renaissance men.

Plus, unlike the great majority of men and women I have worked with since I moved to Hollywood, they genuinely believed in something beyond just advancing themselves in this tough world. The Nixon people genuinely believed in the Constitution. They wanted Americans to be as free as possible within the limits of the law and of the species. They wanted men and women to have equal opportunities. In all my time in the Nixon world, I never heard one word of mockery or derision of women's abilities or qualities as human and political creatures of God.

Without getting any meaningful credit for it, the Nixon people at every level advanced women to the highest levels of responsibility. Anne Morgan and Ute Debus, the top managers of the research department, were greatly respected. (Anne went on to be a major lawyer in Washington and still is.) Professor Whitman, a member of the Council of Economic Advisers, was the first such member. As noted above, the Nixon administration did not make a huge deal over it.

The two speechwriters I worked most closely with, John R. Coyne Jr. and Aram Bakshian Jr., were (as also noted earlier) astonishing geniuses. They were also well informed on a scale I have never seen since. I have stayed in touch with them since I joined in 1973 and am endlessly baffled by their talent and dedication to the nation. John is a Marine, and his commitment—his life-and-death commitment—to the nation is an endless inspiration. Aram went on to be, among many other achievements, President Reagan's chief speechwriter—and it showed in Mr. Reagan's fine addresses. He wrote frequently for high-end literary magazines. Every word of his, just like every word of John's, is artfully placed. Every piece of theirs is a work of art.

They are two of the most impressive human beings I have ever known. And they cared deeply about the nation. They knew very well that RN had won his place in the Oval Office against the violent opposition of the beautiful people in Washington, New York, Boston, and San Francisco. They knew he had fought his way past the mighty cannon of the leftist media—and yet had won the biggest electoral landslide of the century. The people had spoken.

The speech-writing and research staff did not want to see that election overturned by the media overlords. We worked like demons to keep the president in office. We were not paid much. We did not have limousines. We drove ourselves to work. When

I think of the image that some Americans have of the White House and then think of the reality, I smile. We were civil servants. Hardworking, grateful-to-be-of-service civil servants.

But when I left every night, often with my friend Pat and my Weimaraner, Mary, by my side and got into my tiny, un-air-conditioned Subaru, I felt as if I had done a good day's work. I believed I had served the law.

In addition, as I have noted briefly above, the men and women at the Nixon White House saw absolutely no difference between and among human beings in terms of their rights and responsibilities by race. I had been in the civil rights struggle since high school. Even in 1961 and 1962, I had marched in front of a movie theater in Bethesda, Maryland, that still required that Black patrons be seated in a separate part of the auditorium to view movies.

In college, I had been a working member of the Committee on Racial Equality, or CORE, as it was called. We marched and carried placards in Cambridge, a small city on the Eastern Shore of the Chesapeake Bay in my native state of Maryland. On that march, a pickup truck with Confederate flags had pushed me up against a curb, and I had fallen down and badly cut my backside.

Blood was gushing out of me. A kindly soul took me to a local doctor. He sewed up my wound without any kind of anesthetic at all. That hurt.

I found that at the Nixon White House, there was the same kind of etched-in-blood commitment to the full civil rights of Black men and women.

In the twenty-first century, cries of racism are raised against almost every Republican, but the GOP is still the party that had led the struggle against human bondage. In every case where legislation to free or empower the Black man or woman came up, it was the Southern Democrats who fought against having one class of Americans: first class—regardless of race.

Richard Nixon was an unequivocal, tireless fighter for this principle. He had been as a member of Congress, as a senator, as a veep under General Eisenhower, and as a president. From what I saw as a speechwriter at the White House, RN never even slightly deviated from this motive.

In his later years, RN became something of a foeman against Senator Barry Goldwater (R-AZ). Goldwater had secured the 1964 GOP nomination for president. He had amazingly catchy campaign phrases and a wildly well-applauded nomination speech at a stadium aptly called the Cow Palace outside San Francisco.

"In your heart, you know he's right" was one of his billboard slogans. The slogan meant that although some might have considered him a racist (even then, some seven or more decades ago), you (the ordinary American) knew he was on the right track about race and everything else.

His peroration at the end of his acceptance speech at the Cow Palace—"Moderation in the defense of freedom is no virtue. Extremism in the defense of freedom is no vice!"—brought down the house.

The media world of the beautiful people hated him. The power of the incumbency was overwhelming. Lyndon Johnson and his running mate, Senator Hubert Horatio Humphrey of Minnesota, a genuinely fine human being in almost every way, managed to paint Goldwater as a warrior who would not hesitate to plunge the world into nuclear catastrophe.

Johnson won by a vast landslide. The only states that went for Goldwater and his VP pick, an obscure GOP congressman from Upstate New York named William Miller, were southern states.

Ever after that, the Democrats were able to paint the GOP as an anti-Black, racist political party. It has not even been remotely true, but it has stuck.

In the world of 2023 blood-sport politics, race is injected into every discussion of politics. Decisions are made largely on the basis of how they affect the Black vote. This was simply unknown at the time of Richard Nixon's presidency. To be sure, decisions were made largely on the basis of "Will it play in Peoria?"—that is, how it would affect the ordinary working man or woman, Black or white or Latino or anyone. But no one talked about how Black voters would or would not approve of such a decision. Black voters were important, but racial politics were not the be-all and end-all of political decisions.

Nixon's dislike of Barry Goldwater was mostly because of his reckless words, which haunt the GOP to this day.

I bring this up at this point because one day in the summer of 1974, I was walking down the hall on the first floor of the EOB with my father discussing the deepening crisis of Watergate. Who should we see rounding the northeast corner of that corridor but Mr. Nixon, my friend and idol, moving briskly with another friend and idol, the unbelievably handsome, smart, brave, and rich Peter M. Flanigan, international trade adviser, World War II U.S. Navy carrier pilot, successful investment banker, heir, wit, but mainly a really close pal and confidant of Mr. Nixon, and Roy L. Ash, a genuine genius who had—among many other accomplishments—founded one of the first conglomerates, Litton Industries.

At that time, Ash was director of the Office of Management and Budget, a superagency on top of all other agencies, supervising their projects and their budgets. In a previous conversation, he had told me that he had aspired as a young college graduate to be a branch manager at the Bank of America. Instead, he and Tex Thornton had created a whole new corporate form and become phenomenally rich.

Like Peter Flanigan, he was breathtakingly smart.

These were some of the most mentally gifted human beings it has ever been my pleasure to meet.

Mr. Nixon spoke first and, as I recall, said, "Herb and Ben Stein. A lot of brains under one roof. How are you, Herb? Ben, how is your dog? Julie wants you to take our dogs for a walk."

As I have said before, the fact that Mr. Nixon remembered my name at all, let alone my dog, floored me.

Somehow, the conversation turned to my father and me working together at the White House and how lucky I was to have such an opportunity to work with my dad.

"A lot of sons get to work with their fathers at the family business," RN said. "That's not at all as good as this. Here, the dad is not supervising the son and ordering him around. Here, Roy bosses you both around." He laughed at his own joke (but then don't we all?).

That was only a bit of a laugh because, of course, Mr. Nixon was the boss of all of us, including Roy Ash.

"Mr. President," I said to him, "did you ever work for your father? He was a rancher, wasn't he?"

Mr. Nixon looked serious. "My father had a lot of jobs and small businesses. None of them worked in any serious way. At one time, he had a lemon farm, or maybe you might call it a ranch. I did some work there, of the most trivial kind. It certainly was not like reading Keynes on the economic consequences of the Versailles Treaty, which is probably what Herb had you doing." He said this with a nod at me.

This was unbelievably close to the truth. Eerily.

"Barry Goldwater's family owned some big-time stores in the Phoenix area, and he worked there. He got deluged with government paper work. I think that had something to do with his really severe hatred of government. And he never wanted for money, not even for a dime. That allowed him to feel only the most modest amount of commiseration for those without money who needed government help."

We all smiled knowingly, as if we knew something.

"Goldwater never even remotely knew poverty. Neither did your family, Peter. But I did. I knew that we had to be really careful with how much food out of our cupboard we ate every night. Were you ever in that situation, Herb? Was your father ever in business?"

"My father had a few very small businesses," my pop said. "None of them at all successful. He was a skilled tool and die maker at Ford Motor in the 1920s. But he was unemployed for almost all of the Great Depression."

Mr. Nixon smiled knowingly and ruefully. "It changes you to know the possibility of losing your house or your steady meals," Mr. Nixon said.

"That's incredibly hard on human beings," I said to our little group. "Especially when they're Black and have all the problems

of being Black. They don't grow up with any security at all, and
it affects their whole outlook on life."

"And especially if the father is absent and the mother is the
breadwinner and she's stressed and maybe on dope as well. A
young man like you, Ben. At Yale. You never knew even a little
tiny bit the possibility of missing a meal," said Mr. Nixon.

(Again, how did he know I went to Yale Law School?)

"That's something too many of our representatives in Congress don't know. That's why they fight spending on antipov-
erty programs. And they rightly say that half of the money we
spend is wasted," added Mr. Nixon. "But it's like what Herb
here said about defense spending: 'If they waste half of it, give
them twice as much.'"

(How did he know my father had said that on some TV news
panel show?)

"A Republican senator who grew up rich and speaks con-
temptuously about people who can't make it on their own in
the free enterprise system is just not a decent person. A real
leader, whether he's at the county council or the state legislature or the Senate, has to have real empathy for everyone. If he
doesn't, or if she doesn't, it bounces back on the whole party.

"It's amazing, and it's quite a neat trick, but Nelson Rocke-
feller, whose last name is a synonym for 'rich,' manages to sell it
to voters that he really gives a damn about them even if they're
poor. He has some amazing PR people.

"Just like JFK. He could not have cared less about people
who were not rich or articulate—unless he could sleep with
them. But he managed to get it across that he cared for them a
lot. And LBJ. A brilliant man. People think because he has big
feet and sounded like a cowboy that he was a dope.

"Not at all. On a salary of about twelve thousand a year, and the shameless use of political party power, he managed to put together an empire of TV and radio stations worth about a hundred million dollars. And when he took office after Kennedy was murdered, he could not have cared less about Black Americans.

"But once the political tides shifted, he was the Black man's new best friend. And he did something about it. His civil rights acts changed America in a fundamental way. The Fifteenth Amendment allowed Black Americans to vote, but local political offices essentially kept them out of the voting booth. Or else they lynched potential voters.

"That was the Democratic Party. And FDR came along and told people that he was the little man's new best friend, and he didn't lift a finger for Black people. Eleanor? Yes. A real pioneer for Black people's rights. In a way, America's greatest woman leader, without any elected office. A brave woman.

"We in the Republican Party need a woman like her. It's really unfortunate that we don't have a Republican Eleanor Roosevelt. And it's not because they don't exist in the GOP. I've seen them. I've met them, right here in this hallway.

"Anne Armstrong. She could be president. Yes, she's rich. So what? She's a dynamic speaker at party gatherings. She brings men and women to their feet with affection. Why can't we have women like her seriously competing to have the nod? I talk to Julie and Tricia almost every day. They've got the brains to do it. Both of them.

"Ben, you know Julie pretty well. Have you suggested she run for office?"

"I am embarrassed to say I have not," I said.

"You should," the president said. "Why haven't you?"

"Sir, I will," I said, and I meant it.

"She'll have a bad political name now," Mr. Nixon said. "But she's as smart as a whip. She can overcome her last name."

"It's the best possible name," my father said. "It's the name of a peacemaker."

At that Mr. Nixon gave a buddy-buddy punch in the shoulder to my father. My father looked shocked indeed and laughed. Mr. Nixon laughed too.

"Okay. Back to the mineshaft," Mr. Nixon said and walked off down the hall in whatever direction he had come from.

Then he stopped and turned around and called out to me: "Call Julie and offer to take her and her dogs for a walk if you're not too busy."

"Mr. President, it would be my honor," I said, and I meant it.

"Wow, Ben," my pop said as Mr. Nixon and his colleagues rounded a corner. "Remember this afternoon. An economist made a president laugh."

CHAPTER NINE

AU REVOIR: A MEDIA COUP D'ETAT AND THE WORST DAY EVER IN AMERICAN HISTORY

Time passed, as it does inevitably until it stops. My father and I walked around the South Lawn of the White House and talked about how bleak the situation looked for Mr. Nixon. I was terribly worried for him and his program for peace. I was not worried for my father. His name and reputation in his field were already secure. He had been offered many positions and had accepted one at the University of Virginia Department of Economics, plus many other jobs, including one as a columnist on the *Wall Street Journal*'s board of contributors and another as a senior fellow at the American Enterprise Institute and another as a director of Reynolds Metals and another as a director at a Wall Street investment bank called L. F. Rothschild, Unterberg, Towbin. (Supposedly the model for the opening scenes in the movie *The Wolf of Wall Street*.) They were the honest ones, not the evil crooks at Stratton Oakmont.

But I was terrified about my future. My friend, Pat, had talked me into buying a very modest home in a great neighborhood called Wesley Heights. The area had been restricted against Jews until the 1965 Civil Rights Act. The small print on the deed still showed that the property could not be transferred to "Hebrews" or "Negroes."

You would fall to the floor laughing if you knew how little I paid for it back in 1974. Still, it was a major stretch for me, especially if I was about to lose my job at the White House and if I were blacklisted as a Nixon henchman in those evil days and thus unable to get a decent job.

I was fearful about Mr. Nixon, and I was fearful about yours truly.

Still, "the mills of the media grind slow, but they grind exceeding small," as the Plutarch saying almost goes. One day after another, newspaper stories appeared smearing even the most modest Nixon official as part of some immense conspiracy. What had I done that would get me indicted and ruined for life? Forgetting was no excuse for the "Ministry of Love" officers overseeing Watergate, to use a reference to George Orwell's *Nineteen Eighty-Four*.

To this day, in the spring of 2023, I still don't know what Nixon did that merited such angry attacks on him. The closest might be that he mused in a vague way about a plan for the head of the CIA to stop the FBI from pursuing the connections between the Nixon reelection campaign and the Watergate "burglars."

This was a bad but small change compared with what other recent presidents have done. He didn't bring call girls into the White House. He didn't ignore warnings of massive sneak attacks by hostile foreign powers. He was not sneering at warnings of Communist spies in the executive branch. He did not subvert the FBI to compel them to lie to Foreign Intelligence Surveillance Act (FISA) courts and other law enforcement entities.

Above all, as far as I was concerned and as I said earlier, he was a hero of biblical proportions for saving Israel.

Nevertheless, there is a phrase about the "madness of crowds," and by the summer of 1974, the madness had reached the point where the pot boiled over.

For a good reason, by July of 1974, I had been transferred from the normal speech-writing staff under Dave Gergen to the tiny workshop of the chief writer for the president, Ray Price. The fellow who was usually there, a young genius named "Tex" Lezar, had gone back to Texas to go to law school. I was considered "ferociously loyal" to Mr. Nixon, as Ray Price put it in his memoirs, and thus trustworthy even in the most difficult moments.

By then, the clouds were heavy and black. I was in my new house with Pat more or less totally broke and cooking the fake beef stroganoff that comes in a Hamburger Helper box. I was scared. With some reason.

In early August, we of the White House staff were called into a huge auditorium in the EOB for a speech by then White House chief of staff, General Alexander Haig. I remember sitting high up in the seats with Aram Bakshian and John Coyne, giggling like high school boys, as General Haig told us he was "a harbinger of horror." Why were we giggling? I don't remember. I just remember thinking that hard times were a-coming.

At the end of his remarks, General Haig showered us White House staff with compliments. He said he had been in combat many times and that the soldiers he had led in combat were no braver than the men and women working for Mr. Nixon. I can well recall a sense of astonishment at this. After all, what issue at an office desk could be anywhere near as frightening as being shot at or being charged at with bayonets?

Still, I was deeply flattered.

As we were walking out, some staffer (there was no press there) asked General Haig if Mr. Nixon was about to resign. I do not recall General Haig's exact reply, but he said that Mr. Nixon was a fighter and would never resign. One of my colleagues, still a close friend almost fifty years on, leaned over and said, "That means he's resigning."

A few months before, that same colleague, a genuine genius named John R. Coyne Jr., who shared the office suite with me and Aram Bakshian Jr., had sat with me at a small Chinese restaurant on F Street NW, just a block from the EOB. He had discussed with me the likely outcomes of the Watergate crisis. I said I saw no way he could avoid being impeached and convicted. The media landslide against him was simply unstoppable.

John, an order of magnitude smarter about politics than I was and am, shook his head politely. "No," he said. "Nixon has always been a good party man. He's not going to lead the party down a road to disaster. He'll resign first and turn it over to Ford, who's a fantastically likable guy. It's a tragedy because Nixon didn't do anything remotely bad enough—in fact, not bad at all—that merits removal from office. But Nixon will do it for the party."

I recall saying to John that considering how flaccid the GOP's defense of RN had been, it would be a miracle of self-abnegation if Nixon resigned for the GOP.

John smiled and shook his head in a gesture that meant "You should be right, but we'll see."

Now, after General Haig's remarks, it looked more and more as if John Coyne had seen the future clearly and I had not.

When I walked into my tiny cubbyhole near Ray Price, after our gathering with General Haig, I noticed a group of people near the desk of Ray's wonderful secretary, Margaret Foote. As I walked by, the group looked friendly and called me by name, and some actually might have patted me on the back.

They walked into Ray's office and did not invite me to join them.

A few minutes later, I had to have a meeting with one of the kindest, most pleasant women I have ever met, Patricia Matson, a high aide to Mrs. Nixon and the salt of the earth.

I took the most direct route to the East Wing, the First Lady's wing, which involved walking through the Diplomatic Reception Room. It is a circular, large, airy room with many historical paintings. I had been to many receptions there and used to meet my parents there to go to religious services in the East Room.

This time, as I walked through that room, I noticed something breathtaking: there were movers in uniforms loading racks of women's clothing—some of it recognizable as Mrs. Nixon's style of clothing—into unmarked medium-sized trucks.

It was a thunderclap. Patti Matson did not discuss it at all, even when I brought it up. She just looked doleful.

The events after that moved with dizzying speed. Even now, some forty-eight or so years later, it all seems like a blur. John Coyne and I discussed it, maybe on the phone, because I have the faintest memory of his being out of town. Aram Bakshian and I discussed it, maybe also on the phone, because I have a memory that he also was out of town at some celebration of a great Austrian composer.

We all agreed that it was the end.

I do not recall what day it was, but I know it was the first week in August 1974, and many Washingtonians were out of the humid, desperately hot city on their vacations.

My next-door neighbor at 4411 Klingle Street NW in Wesley Heights was the Washington correspondent for a large Italian newspaper. I do not recall his name, but I do recall that he told me that it looked as if the Watergate mess was quieting down for the summer, so maybe it was time for him to go back to Italy for a vacation for a week.

I told him that he had better stay in DC.

The next day, I spoke to Julie. She said that Mr. Nixon's hideaway office in the EOB had to be packed up very soon. Only she had a good idea of what had to be packed and where it was to be sent. But she would welcome my company just to visit with her while she packed. She did not say when it would be except that it would be soon.

Then came the announcement over the wires that Mr. Nixon would be giving an important speech the next night. By then, John Coyne was back in his office, and we talked mournfully about the situation that he had so precisely predicted long before. Dave Gergen also convoked a meeting of the speech-writing staff and told them that while he could not tell them what was in the speech because it was all being drafted in Ray Price's shop, he wanted us all to avoid any leaks or any contact with the press at all.

Normally, this would not have been the slightest problem for me, since I knew almost no one in the press. However, this time was different. The one member of the press I knew extremely well was Carl Bernstein. He had been my next-door neighbor since about 1954. He had ridden to fame and fortune through his pursuit of the Watergate scandal.

We had stayed in touch, although he knew me to be the most dogged and devoted Nixon fan and protector on the planet. Carl also knew that I would not under any circumstances say anything secret or negative about Nixon. This had been true since I first met Carl during the height of the McCarthy era. His family hated all the Red hunters, and my family did not like the Reds at all.

Still, Carl knew enough to be discreet in his questions to me, and I never—and I mean *never*—spoke any ill about Nixon. But now Carl was calling to find out what was going on at Nixon land.

I was friendly and so was he, but as always, I said nothing at all about Nixon. (In later years, we discussed him, but Carl and I will never—and I mean *never*—see eye to eye about a man whom I consider a god and Carl considers a criminal.)

I did not give him any answers, but we cheerily said we would stay in touch. (It remains an astonishing fact of my life that Carl and I used to be next-door neighbors as small children and wound up so tightly bound about the key man in my life besides my father, Richard Milhous Nixon. Carl's parents, Alfred and Sylvia Bernstein, were at some point accused of being Communists—actual card-carrying Communists—and maybe they were. But they were wonderful neighbors and friends, just great. Carl had two sisters, Mary and Laura, and they were delightful young women too.)

At some point, my father called to tell me that Mr. Nixon was going to resign the next day in an evening speech. He and my mother would be watching it from their home in Silver Spring, Maryland, and then there would be a speech to the White House staff and the cabinet in the East Room the next morning.

I had seen it coming, but I was in a daze. I did not drink, but for some reason, I went to a nearby liquor store and bought a pint of Black & White Scotch. I don't think I ever even opened the bottle.

In my tiny office in Ray Price's bailiwick, I saw Ray working furiously. I waved to him and asked him if I could do anything. He smiled wanly and shook his head. "You've been great," he said. "Buttoned up on the outside and unbuttoned on the inside." Same words and phrases that Mr. Nixon had spoken to my father early in 1973 when he told him he was being kept on as chair of the CEA, even though there had been many changes in personnel in the White House.

Then he added, "Your idea for the president to apologize was good. It just wasn't Nixon."

I had forgotten that some weeks before, I had suggested to Ray that President Nixon give a speech—and I believe I had written a draft—in which he apologized for whatever wrong he had done. I wanted him to list in a general way the wrongs of other presidents—bringing call girls into the White House; bungling an "invasion" of Castro's Cuba; cooperating with Stalin in enslaving most of Eastern Europe; getting us into a long and horribly bloody war in Korea because of foolishly mangled statements about U.S. defense policy in East Asia, probably arranged by the Left's hero, Alger Hiss; and using a completely phony naval incident in the Tonkin Gulf to get us into the horrible Vietnam War— and then I suggested that he listed his achievements: achieving peace in Vietnam, opening up Red China, reaching a détente with the USSR, and above all, rescuing the very life of Israel.

"I have made mistakes," I had him saying in my draft, "but I have also made some serious steps toward world peace and away from nuclear war. I apologize to the American people for my mistakes. But I ask you to ignore the cries of the press and allow me to stay in office to continue my work for peace."

Ray had thought it was a good speech and recommended it to Mr. Nixon (or so he told me). But Nixon—or maybe it was Haldeman—had simply said something like "Contrition is bullshit." That was the end of that.

I recall watching RN's resignation speech on a simply beautiful, lavishly upholstered couch in Dave Gergen's office, along with Dave; John Coyne; the head of the researchers, Anne Morgan; and my girlfriend, Pat, a wonderful girl who was employed at the Council of Economic Advisers because of the intervention of my father. Life is life, and Pat and I later became estranged. I love her a lot, but she has refused to speak to me for close to fifty years.

"The man who forgives is walking in the footsteps of God," so goes the biblical injunction. Some hear it, and some don't.

I don't remember as much of the speech as I should. I do recall thinking that there still was not much of a reason for RN to resign. His explanation, that Watergate was a distraction from the urgent business of the government and therefore he should remove himself from the equation, was true, to be sure. But it was a long way from the basic truth of the situation: there had been a media coup d'état. (I am reminded endlessly of *Jesus Christ Superstar*, when Christ appears before Pilate. Pilate asks him many questions. Jesus answers, "I look for truth and find that I get banned." Pilate replies, "But what is truth? Is it unchanging law? We all have truths. Are mine the same as yours?")

Naturally, I was crying by the time RN finished. My fellow speechwriters and Anne Morgan sympathized with me.

After the speech, Pat and I walked down the hall to my tiny office next to Ray Price's. Ray shook hands with me gravely. "You're a good man, Ben," he said. He was a much, much better man.

Margaret Foote, Ray's secretary, whom I thought of then as old, saw my tears and stood up and gripped me by my shoulders. Of course, she was far younger than I am now. "Don't let the bastards see you cry, Ben," she said. "Don't give them that much satisfaction."

I loved her then and now.

Margaret handed me a slip of paper. It was a pass to the East Room, where RN would be giving his farewell to the White House staff speech the next morning. It was sent over by Julie, as I have said and will say to the end of my days, a genuine saint.

Pat and I awoke early the next morning and went to the White House. Pat, an extremely beautiful girl, looked even more beautiful than usual. She had been the most loyal of loyal women.

The room was packed. Pat and I stood off to the right of the Nixon family. My parents were seated in the first row, as close to Mr. Nixon as anyone could be. Mr. Nixon knew well that my father and especially my mother would have done anything for him. My mother would have literally done anything for him. This is not a figure of speech.

Mr. Nixon's speech can be found anywhere. There are videos of him all over the internet. Pat and I can be seen close up in a couple of frames. I'm much thinner and younger there, and I'm crying and chewing gum at the same time. I don't remember why I was chewing gum. My then ex-wife, who has since been my wife for roughly a total of sixty years, was in Lafayette

Square across the street. Her fellow demonstrators were chanting "Jail to the chief." Times change.

Nixon gave the best speech I had ever heard him give. Without notes, he said that he had been to far grander houses for national chief executives. But the White House, he said, was the best house because it had the best people in it. He talked about the chefs and the ushers and then about high officials and cabinet members. My mother, God bless her soul, was sobbing uncontrollably. I never saw her so upset. My father, a stoic man, looked as if he were about to be shot. When my mother died before he did, he was the most upset—not to say "demolished"—he had ever been. But next after that was his response to RN's resignation. My father made no bones about it. Other economists at the White House might have been dispassionate about their work. My father did put "science" first. But economics is a vague science at best. Karl Marx called it a "bourgeois pseudoscience." My father recognized its shortcomings. But he recognized that he loved Richard Nixon more than he had ever loved anyone other than my mother, my sister, and me. He was ashen at RN's farewell speech.

Pat was staggered. Her father had died when she was about ten. She had transferred her love of an older man to my father and to me and to Mr. Nixon. She would have done anything for him. She was as fine a human being as has ever walked the earth. Her loyalty was never even slightly in question as far as RN was concerned. When she walked with me back to the EOB, she walked with a dignity, solemnity, and sorrow such as I have seen on a woman only one other time: in a video of the late British monarch standing in respect for the fallen in World War II in a ceremony that was (I believe) in

1970 at the twenty-fifth anniversary of Victory in Europe Day. When Pat stood next to me at RN's farewell speech, she was quivering.

Mr. Nixon talked about how modest his childhood had been. He talked about how he had learned that you have to be in the lowest valley before you can appreciate the splendor of the mountaintop. Julie, Tricia, Ed Cox, David Eisenhower, and, of course, the paragon of women, Pat Nixon, stood behind him. They looked as if they were suffering terribly, and they were.

RN talked about how his father had never been rich, but he was a great man because he did his job and took care of his family. He talked about his mother and what a great woman she was. She had taken care of RN's brother as he was dying of TB. At the same time, she had worked caring for other children with TB to earn the family's living. My heart was just breaking. It was the inner thoughts of a great man standing before an audience of men and women who loved him in that East Room and a nation split about him, a nation whipped up to a frenzy of hate by a media that had become the modern-day equivalent of the Ministry of Love in Orwell's *Nineteen Eighty-Four*.

As far as I am aware, no president has ever spoken as candidly and deeply about his family and his feelings in front of a mass audience. I am not sure that any national leader has ever spoken as candidly about his deepest feelings about himself before a worldwide audience as Richard Nixon did on that hot, muggy August day in 1974.

We saw a man so powerful that he could have ordered nuclear war and basically end life on the planet. And here he was, stripped naked and confessing his sins—even sins he had never committed—to a nest of vipers called the national media.

Then he switched to a different note: regret over a lost love, basically taken from an Edith Piaf song called "Non, je ne regrette rien." Only in this case, the lost love was the United States of America.

"This is not good-bye," he said to us as if he had been channeling Madame Piaf. "The French have a word for it: 'Au revoir.' We'll see you again." Of course, there was a lot more to it than that. There always is when a love affair ends.

Then he left. He walked down the stairs, through the Diplomatic Reception Room, and out to Marine One, the president's helicopter. He stood at the door and waved good-bye. We were all out on a balcony waving at him.

I went over and hugged my mother and father and stared at the astounding sight. By that time, I was just a ball of tears. "A media coup d'état," my mother said again. I still sometimes watch the video of Mr. Nixon's farewell speech. I never saw my mother so brokenhearted before or since.

Then Marine One's rotors began to rotate, and the aircraft flew away, and so Mr. Nixon went off into immortality.

I said good-bye to my mother and father, who walked away in what I would now call a "trudging motion." Then Pat and I walked west toward the door to West Executive Avenue holding hands.

Fred Dent, secretary of commerce and a friend, came up behind me and patted me on the back. "It'll be all right, Ben," he said. "It'll be all right." That was the kind of spirit at the RN White House. A band of brothers and sisters. I've never worked anywhere like it before or since.

I went over to RN's hideaway office. Amazingly, Julie was already there packing Republican elephants that had been given to the president over the years.

Her eyes were moist, so I did not attempt to say anything beyond "The worst day ever in American history. Is there anything I can do to help?"

She smiled gamely and motioned to a chair for me to sit on. As I did, I saw that next to the armrest of the chair was a Xerox of a page from a book of Lincoln's writings. This one was an extremely well-known entry.

It was about how God had blessed America by placing us between two great oceans so that no foreign enemy could get across them to invade. (This was obviously written before anyone dreamed of an invasion from farther south in our hemisphere by millions of people on foot, waved in by an administration that wanted to demolish the America we know and love.) If America were to be ruined, wrote the Great Emancipator, we would have to do it to ourselves by dividing and making war upon ourselves.

The writing was cruelly apropos. I watched Julie in silence for about twenty minutes. Then the phone rang, and Julie picked it up with great excitement. She was obviously speaking to her parents, so I got up, waved discreetly to her, and walked away.

Pat had already walked back to her office down the hall from my father's office on the third floor. I walked back to my microscopic office next to Ray Price's office. Margaret Foote was not at her desk, and Ray's door was closed. I moved a few trivial belongings from that tiny office to my much bigger office next to John Coyne and Aram Bakshian, genuine geniuses and friends in a dark time.

John walked into my office silently and handed me an article (Xeroxed, of course, as everything was in those days) by the great Arthur Miller about Nixon.

It was an extremely sympathetic piece about RN's last weeks and days. It talked about how in the end, RN admitted what presidents of the United States are never supposed to admit: that he had made small and large mistakes (I personally thought that he had not made any large mistakes) and that he had failed to tell the truth about them.

In the end, Miller, no novice at making large mistakes and paying the price, said that what RN had admitted to was that he was "one of us," just an ordinary person who made mistakes—even if he did have his own helicopter.

I read the article. Then I called Pat. She came down with a plate of cookies that the research staff of the Council of Economic Advisers had made for the occasion.

The end of an era.

CHAPTER TEN

CALIFORNIA PART 2: A DREAM JOB

Back to topic A. I was soon officially moved back to my old office with my pals (still my pals almost fifty years down the road) John R. Coyne Jr. and Aram Bakshian Jr. We got a new speech-writing boss, whose name I no longer recall, although the wonderful Dave Gergen continued to be our day-to-day boss. Gergen was not only a supersmart man but also a kind-hearted man and a good friend from then until now. The atmosphere at the staff offices was amazingly good, except at my office.

I had the facility to call the techies who controlled such things and have them put up on my TV set Mr. Nixon's farewell speech. There was Mr. Nixon. There was his family behind him. There were my mother and father sobbing just a few feet from Mr. Nixon. And there I was, sitting in my office sobbing in tune.

Unknown to me, the White House Communications Agency that sent out these "rebroadcasts" was also sending them to every other TV in the WH complex. This was to have serious implications for me.

My father was still chairman of the CEA, and my friend Pat (as fine a human as there has ever been) was still up there on the third floor.

For some reason, I was given more weighty speeches to write than ever before. Except for the searing burden of missing Mr. Nixon, my life was good.

Mr. Ford and my father had been friends for decades, ever since Mr. Ford started inviting my father to testify at congressional hearings where a Republican was needed at short notice. Mr. Ford, a thorough gentleman, was grateful, and family always meant everything to him. Maybe that had something to do with why I started getting invites to far more cabinet meetings than I ever had gotten under RN.

The cabinet meetings were fascinating. Instead of the superbraino geniuses (at least as they saw themselves) we had in that room under RN, we had a much more Main Street bunch of men and women of steady habits. They couldn't have been friendlier or more down to earth. A small-city Rotary Club meeting was how I saw them, even smaller than the ones I attended (rarely, to be sure) under RN.

I was still in frequent touch with Julie. My father was on an extremely close basis with RN. Julie and I had an idea at one time of having a TV chat show. An extraordinarily kind and thoughtful man at Warner TV, Eddie Bleier, tried to get it going. He had been college roommates with Bill Safire, the supercolumnist for the *New York Times* editorial page. Safire did not get fired for defending RN to the last, unlike what would happen in the world of 2023. And his enthusiasm for Nixon spilled over to Eddie Bleier, who (like many men) just loved Julie. Despite his great affection for Julie and her proposed talk show, Eddie Bleier was never able to get it going beyond an outline that Julie and I wrote and for which I was paid a hearty thank-you.

I also helped Julie get an agent, the redoubtable David Obst, for her to write and sell a book. She was a superb writer, but then you must remember I love everything about her and David. She wrote a book about famous women in public life and a spectacularly good book about her mother, the great Pat Nixon.

Life was going on fairly well after RN's leave-taking. He and I had a frequent and cordial typewritten—or more usually, handwritten by RN and typed by me—correspondence.

Then one day I got a call from Donald Rumsfeld. I had known him for some time because he was head of the Office of Economic Opportunity (OEO), the umbrella organization for LBJ's War on Poverty. I was a lawyer in the Office of Legal Services, the entity that provided free legal services in the civil arena to people who could not afford Perry Mason. I often had conferences with Mr. Rumsfeld and found him to be a friendly, slightly brusque boss.

I also knew Mr. Rumsfeld because he had traveled around the nation with my father as my pop explained to the world the workings of RN's wage-price controls as set forth after his momentous meetings at Camp David in August 1971. My father had told me just a few days before Mr. Rumsfeld's call to me that he considered Don Rumsfeld his closest friend. Mr. Rumsfeld was, at the time of this call, chief of staff at the White House.

"Ben," Mr. Rumsfeld asked cheerily, "how are you enjoying your life in the Ford White House?"

"Very much indeed," I said.

"Well, I'm afraid you're going to have to make some changes soon, because we're letting most of the 'old Nixon hands' go to greener pastures."

"I'm stunned," I said as I felt faint. "I've gotten nothing but compliments on my work, including some from Mr. Ford himself."

"I know," Rumsfeld said. "We all are happy with you. But we want a more Ford and less Nixon staff. The communications people tell me that you're always showing Nixon's farewell speech on the TVs here, and it's depressing people."

So much for being my father's best friend.

During the 2016 presidential campaign, Mr. Trump repeatedly referred to the "deep state" and the "Washington swamp" of permanent employees and power players in the nation's capital.

I guess I was lucky enough to be part of that swamp. Mr. Rumsfeld solicitously told me that if I could not find a job in the private sector within a few weeks, he would find me a good job, a "deputy assistant secretary of transportation" or some such to keep the wolf away from the door.

But my parents had been part of the swamp for decades. I told my parents about the call from Mr. Rumsfeld. Within hours, my mother had found me a fine job at Hill & Knowlton, a powerful Washington PR firm; another one at the Department of Health and Human Services, where her dear friend, Jane Weinberger, the wife of the HHS secretary Caspar "Cap" Weinberger, had a lot of sway; and others besides. My father had extracted a promise from Mr. Rumsfeld to open up the golden doors of the "bureaucracy" to me, and they were opened.

But most alluring of all was a conversation I had with Bob Bartley, the legendary editor of the editorial page of the *Wall Street Journal*. I had been writing freelance pieces for the editorial page of the *Wall Street Journal* for about four years. These were mostly pieces about the political and sociopolitical views of television shows and movies.

I found it compelling that TV shows and movies had standard themes that were often different from real life. For example, if there were a murder in a city background, in real life, the culprits would likely be men from nonwhite homes, often men with prior criminal records for the same or similar crimes.

But in TV cop shows, the perps would be the local bank president or the principal of the high school. The writers of the shows or movies were at pains at all times to show that the whole face of society was fraudulent and that the so-called respectable people were in reality killers and thieves and rapists.

I wrote a number of columns for the editorial page of the *Wall Street Journal* explaining how TV drama worked along these lines. Bob Bartley liked them, and when I told him I was being cut loose by the White House, he offered me a job immediately. The job would be to write one column a week, mostly about the subterranean political content of TV shows and movies, and also to assign freelancers to review books and plays and ballets and operas and art exhibitions.

It was in many ways a dream job for a writer. The only problems were that I had to move to New York, a city I love but also an expensive city, and my job paid modestly indeed. The working quarters for us writers for the editorial page were Spartan to the point of humiliation. They were far below what I had experienced at the Federal Trade Commission or the OEO.

However, there was an immense plus. At that point in the history of print journalism, the *Wall Street Journal* was kind and generous enough to send us ink-stained wretches all over the world—and in first class, at that.

While we were covering shows and showings in New York, we were expected to take the subway, and in those days in the mid-1970s, the subways were not air-conditioned and smelled horribly of homeless people's smell, but flying to LA first class was opulent and great. I made it a point to find as many events to cover and Hollywood power players to interview as I possibly could.

Very soon, I had made friends with a number of big wheels in Hollywood. They were all happy to be on good terms with a columnist for the *Wall Street Journal*. One of them was the giant sitcom potentate Norman Lear. He had read and enjoyed a piece I wrote about how *All in the Family* was supposed to make the viewers loathe the working class as Neanderthal Nixon lovers but instead had made them love Nixon and "hard hats" more than ever.

Al Burton, Norman Lear's primary paladin, played an episode of Lear's *Mary Hartman, Mary Hartman* for me at a conference of TV critics in Aspen. The other critics hated it, but I thought it was a work of genius. Al had brought his wife to Aspen. Al and I became the closest of friends. (His wife, a leftist of the first degree, right out of Beverly Hills, a real Nixon hater, became a close friend too. We were still close friends until the late summer of 2022, although Al, by far the best friend I ever had, entered immortality in 2019.) I wrote about Mary Hartman in those glowing terms in the *Wall Street Journal*. The piece attracted so much attention that Norman Lear was able to sell the show into syndication on the same morning that the piece appeared in the *Wall Street Journal*.

"Selling it into syndication" generally—not always—is immensely lucrative. It can be far more lucrative than selling it directly to the network, which is what Norman Lear originally wanted to do. Norman Lear was grateful.

He asked if we could have lunch together the next time he was in New York. We had lunch at the Italian Pavilion and had a lot of laughs. Norman, a first-class World War II U.S. Army Air Forces hero and an authentic cultural genius, had been a severe enemy of Richard Nixon. He had not held it to be possible that he could like anyone who loved Nixon.

But Norman and I hit it off like army buddies. By the end of the lunch, Norman told me he had never met a conservative who had a great (according to him) sense of humor. He wanted me to quit my job at the *Wall Street Journal* and fly out to Hollywood and be a consultant on a forthcoming show about a Jane Fonda type who falls in love with a Bill Buckley type.

The job paid a whopping $600 per week. At the time, it seemed like an astonishing amount of money. It was easy-peasy work, and I could lease a Mercedes-Benz convertible instead of taking the humid Seventh Avenue IRT (Interborough Rapid Transit). I would work for two big-time TV sitcom professionals, Bob Schiller and Bob Weiskopf. I met them and liked them immediately. Both of them were extreme leftists but also extremely great guys, patriots, and talented at a high level.

I signed up for the job. It was only guaranteed to last a few months, whereas at the *Wall Street Journal*, I had something like a lifetime tenure. I remember thinking that I was a fool to risk my future on the odds in Hollywood, a notoriously risky spot on the map of careers.

Still, I loved Hollywood and was assured by Al Burton that I would "make it" here and that I need not fear.

I left my beautiful apartment on West Sixty-Sixth Street. I gave away most if not all my furniture to a Russian Jewish immigrant. He was a stout but extremely strong man. In those days (June 1976), color televisions were incredibly heavy. But he picked it up with his hands and hustled out the door with it. He likewise took every movable item in the apartment.

This was what Russian Bolshevism had done to the Russian people. They were starved for material goods. And they were the saddest redneck tenant farmers, whom I had often seen because my grandfather-in-law in Idabel, Oklahoma, had several tenant farmers (or sharecroppers) who lived better than most Russians. My wife and I often went out with him (Big Daddy, as we called him) to collect rents, sometimes paid in coins. The people in those shacks lived like Marie Antoinette compared with that Russian Jewish immigrant who took my TV. Luckily, they did not all die like Marie Antoinette.

On June 30, 1976, I went out to JFK with David Obst. Together we flew first class nonstop to LAX. In those days, even coach was luxurious travel, but first class was something else: there were empty rows where I could stretch out and sleep, the food was good, and we could smoke and even take drugs. My life opened up like a rose.

Al Burton, the absolutely finest person on the planet except for my wife, was my boss and contact at Norman Lear's TV sitcom factory. Al had arranged for a long black Cadillac limousine to meet me at baggage claim. In it were three beautiful young actresses wearing short shorts and matching T-shirts that said, in bold print, "I'm Benjy's." They clustered around me while a photographer took photos.

Of course, nowadays such a thing would not be even remotely considered. It would be thought of as "sexist" and demeaning to women. But the young actresses got paid for a day's work, they made friends at the studio, and we were all happy.

Now the airline cabins, even in first class, are pigpens. The food, even in what is laughingly called "priority," is actual pig swill. The airports are choked with the sickening smell of skunk-flavored marijuana. There are fights with fists and base-ball bats on the sidewalks outside baggage claim, at least at LAX, and no police at all to keep things safe. The collapse of civility has been completed at LAX.

When I was at the *Wall Street Journal*, I had become close friends with a genius music mogul and publicist, head of Roll-ing Stones Records, a fabulously lucid and amusing fellow named Earl McGrath. Through Earl, I became pals with my idol, Joan Didion, and her phenomenally gifted husband, a writer named John Gregory Dunne. They were essayists, nov-elists, and screenwriters. They were also at the hub of a Holly-wood clockwork that most newcomers would sell their souls to be a part of.

But through Earl and Joan and John and Norman Lear, I got into that hub immediately. The center of that hub was a small talent agency called the Ziegler, Diskant, and Roth Agency, named for its principals, Evarts ("Ev") Ziegler and George Diskant. They also had a partner named Steve Roth, an heir, as so many people in Hollywood are. Hollywood's first worship is money. If you come there with money in your pockets, you are way ahead of the game. You are immediately a deity. No bus-boys, waitresses, or Uber drivers are barred from trying for the brass ring. But if you come here with a name associated with money, you are instantly nobility, of greater or lesser stature. You already have the brass ring. Norman Lear had mistakenly assumed that the Steins were all major Wall Street players, and perhaps his kindness and respect for me had some small basis in that mistake, but probably not. Norman was a genuinely great guy in all regards.

(By fate, as time passed, my father did become something meaningful on Wall Street, but never on the level Norman had believed. My father at one time had been the single largest stockholder outside the Reynolds family of Reynolds Metals fame. He was only such a large stockholder because as a member of the board of directors of Reynolds, he had been responsible for the employees' pension funds. That involved the ownership of millions of shares of Reynolds Metals, but only titularly and temporarily. That was enough to give the impression that he was rich and that I was rich. I attempted to correct the impression at every opportunity, but still the impression stuck. It was an immensely helpful false impression. By being "rich" and by being a pal of Earl McGrath, again, I was immediately "in the club," as one might say.)

My first stop as I left LAX was at the Ziegler, Diskant, and Roth Agency. It was a miraculous, life-changing visit. Ziegler and Diskant were stupendously self-confident men. They gave the impression that they could make me a superstar almost at will. I especially hit it off with George Diskant, as a devout fan of stock market investing as I am. George was later to introduce me to the wonderful world of Berkshire Hathaway and Warren Buffett. Mr. Buffett and I became friends and still communicate frequently.

Then I started my routine of working for Norman Lear as a consultant on how "conservatives" think and even how "we" talk. It was pleasant, easy work. I'm not even sure I would call it "work." The only slightly awkward part of the gig was when we taped the shows of *All's Fair* in front of a live audience. Messrs. Schiller and Weiskopf introduced the main performers, the writers, and the directors.

I was introduced as "our resident fascist." To successful people in Hollywood, any Republican was a fascist. It wasn't quite as funny to me, who had three cousins murdered by the Nazis.

I protested to Messrs. Schiller and Weiskopf. They laughed.

My point is not at all that they were mean-spirited people. They were fine people. My point is that to Hollywood people, political conservatives are such an alien breed that they might as well be Martians. A man or woman who favors the right-to-work law might as well be a stormtrooper for Hitler. In the meantime, I just laughed and scratched and collected my memories and my $600 per week. I also observed and got into the Hollywood lifestyle, which was mostly immensely pleasant: working on a novel I had already sold and mostly finished called *On the Brink*. It was about a hyperinflationary catastrophe with overwhelming, Weimar-level inflation sweeping across the nation and the world. I was also working on a diary of my super-sybaritic lifestyle, which meant I ate at the "in" restaurants like Ma Maison and the Palm and Spago, dated starlets, and wrote and published many, many newspaper and magazine articles, mostly about economic policy and also about life in Hollywood.

I also had many friends that I regularly had lunch with, almost always at the Palm. In fact, at that time of my life, I had far more friends than I ever had since. Hollywood has become strictly "restricted" against political conservatives. In those days, politics rarely even came up at lunch or dinner.

I soon found that I had so much time on my hands that I could easily make time to see Richard Nixon in San Clemente whenever I wanted. I quickly made time.

CHAPTER ELEVEN

A MEMORABLE BIRTHDAY PARTY
AT THE WESTERN WHITE HOUSE

By this time, it was midsummer. That meant that Julie Eisenhower's birthday was coming up. I got a call from Julie inviting me to a birthday party for her at the beautiful home of Jack and Helen Drown in Palos Verdes. The Drowns had been friends with Richard and Patricia Nixon since wartime and had not skipped a beat in that friendship no matter how bad things had gotten during the Watergate era. "It's just going to be a small party," Julie said. "But see if you have time to come."

I had already visited Mr. Nixon at his office at what had been called the Western White House. It was a modest office whose main features were a mass of American and military flags neatly arranged around his desk, a small collection of Republican elephants, and, best of all, Mr. Nixon's beloved Irish Setter, King Timahoe, invariably lying at Mr. Nixon's feet wherever RN was sitting.

This party was going to be something quite different—a social affair with food and drink. I did not have a driver in those days and there was no Waze or GPS. With the help of my trusty *Thomas Guide*, I found my way to the site. I got there just moments before Mr. and Mrs. Nixon came in. He was kind enough to greet me right away.

I could see that this was going to be a small event. There were only a few chairs spread about in the living room and at the dining table.

Mr. Nixon's face looked the most relaxed I had ever seen it. He shook hands with Jack Drown, and Jack asked him what he wanted to drink. RN mentioned a mixed drink, like a Scotch and water, but my memory of what it was exactly is inexact.

"Make it a light one," Mr. Nixon said to Mr. Drown, slapping him on the shoulder in a buddy-buddy way. "You always make them too strong."

Mrs. Nixon shook hands with me and laughed. "It's good to meet you at last," she said. "Julie has told us so much about you that it's"—she paused for a moment, looking for the right word—"nauseating."

It was said in a lighthearted, cheerful way, and we all laughed, including me.

Julie refused any kind of mixed drink or anything at all except water. Mrs. Nixon took Julie's hands in hers and said to us, "Julie isn't feeling that well. She ate too much fresh fruit for lunch. It doesn't agree with her."

"I feel the same way," I said.

Mr. Nixon held Julie's hand and held it in an affectionate way. Then he looked at me and asked if I had seen President Ford's U.S. bicentennial celebration events and how I liked them.

"They were fine," I said noncommittally.

"It was fine," Mr. Nixon said. "But he could have done it better. He is a great man. But he shouldn't have frittered the event up on a bunch of small speeches. Should have really worked on it and given one big speech. A speech that Americans would have remembered for years. He should have gone up to Camp David and hidden away and worked on it for a week."

"Why didn't he do that?"

None of us had a clue and so none of us said anything.

Mr. Nixon started to talk about the upcoming election. "It looks like Carter has it locked up. But who will he choose for vice president?" He paused and then answered his own question: "I think it has to be Mondale. He looks good on camera. He's Catholic."

"Why not Muskie?" I asked.

"Too old," Mr. Nixon said. "Speaking of which, it's amazing how close Reagan got to winning the nomination. The Republican Party is changing. The base is changing. Someday some outsider will pick that up and get the nomination and be president."

(This reminds me of two anecdotes about Ronald Reagan and Donald Trump that I will insert here. I apologize; I know it's out of order. In 1973, New England Brahmin Archibald Cox was the Watergate special prosecutor. Mr. Nixon deemed that Cox was too zealous and that he overstepped his mandate too often.)

(Richard Nixon consulted his top people at the DOJ. They told him that Cox was arrogant and impossible to work with in a constructive way. Most of them suggested that he be fired. The attorney general, another socialite, a man named Elliot Richardson, disagreed and wanted him kept on. He said he would resign in protest if Cox were fired.)

(Mr. Nixon consulted with other lights of the GOP, including Governor Ronald Reagan of our beloved sunny California. They generally urged Mr. Nixon to fire Cox.)

(On October 20, 1973, Mr. Nixon did fire Cox. Sure enough, Attorney General Richardson immediately resigned. He packed a small briefcase and left, escorted out the door by FBI agents.)

(Mr. Nixon then appointed a well-liked lawyer who had been deputy attorney general, William Ruckelshaus, to be attorney general. Mr. Ruckelshaus immediately, within minutes, resigned. His wife had come to loathe Washington, DC, so the decision was easy.)

(In a stroke of brilliance, Mr. Nixon then appointed Robert Bork, who had been solicitor general of the DOJ, to be attorney general. Professor Bork had been my professor of constitutional law at Yale. He was a stone-solid genius of law. He was a stunningly bright jewel of legal analysis, as much of a breakthrough as any teacher I have ever had.)

(When the story exploded onto the front pages of newspapers the day later, Governor Reagan called Mr. Nixon and said, regarding the previous two days' events, "That's acting like a president." That call cheered Mr. Nixon considerably.)

(The second anecdote, about RN and Trump, concerns a call I had with someone close to Mr. Nixon but not necessarily related. She told me that some years before, RN wanted to move from San Clemente to New York City so he could be near his children and grandchildren. There are several co-ops in fancy neighborhoods in New York. Co-op owners are part of a committee for the building and can reject or blackball a member for any reason, including being too Black or too Jewish or too gay.)

(Several such committees told RN, a former president, that he was not welcome. Donald Trump heard about it. Mr. Trump

contacted RN and told him that he was always welcome anywhere at any time in any dwelling in which Mr. Trump had
any degree of control. Mr. Nixon and his whole family were
deeply impressed.)

(I was damned impressed.)

Mr. Nixon (we're back at Julie's birthday party now) asked
me how I thought the bicentennial celebrations went. I told
him I thought they went well, especially the tall ships in New
York Harbor. "But I thought the Israelis celebrated it better than we did. They knew it was life or death for them. They
showed real emotion."

"Exactly," Mr. Nixon agreed. "Why don't we do things like
that anymore?"

No one had an answer.

The talk turned to Entebbe because Mr. Nixon said that
Israel knew how to do almost everything better than anyone
else. He was wildly impressed that Israel had been able to fly
about twenty-five hundred miles to rescue the Jews and everyone else that the Palestinian hijackers had managed to take to
the capital of Uganda. "Can you imagine how surprised Idi
Amin must have been?"

(At that time, Idi Amin was the dictator of Uganda.)

Nixon shook his head. "Amin?" he asked the room. "He's just
a goddamn asshole. A goddamn cannibal asshole. He'd eat his
own mother. Christ! He'd eat his own grandmother."

We all nodded in agreement. No Idi Amin fans in that room
and one for-sure Jew.

RN then went on to the subject of African leaders. "Yes,
always give them an advantage because they're Black. They've
suffered because they're Black. Give them a break, always.

Certainly. But when they start acting like assholes, you don't
coddle them and tell them they're doing just fine. That's insult-
ing them. It's telling them that we don't expect them to act
right just because they're Black.

"Black people can be marvelous. You used to work for Bob
Brown, right, Ben? Smart as a whip." (Again, I wondered how
Mr. Nixon knew about my insignificant part-time job for Bob
Brown, assistant to the president for minority affairs or some-
thing similar. It had been a small job, but there were those who
loved it.)

"Why can't African leaders be that smart?" Mr. Nixon continued. "They're just a mess, and no sooner is one kicked out
than a new one even worse appears, and then we have to act
friendly to him."

David Eisenhower answered and asked simultaneously,
"Sure, but what can we do about it?"

Mr. Nixon looked sad and said, "Good question."

At that point, I asked Mr. Nixon why Kurt Waldheim, then
secretary general of the UN General Assembly, had criticized
Israel for rescuing its hostages in Entebbe.

"Why?" Mr. Nixon asked with a wry smile. "Waldheim?
Because he's an asshole, and the UN is full of goddamn assholes. That's why."

No one disagreed. We went on to a new subject: the election.
"Carter might be very good because he's very good on defense,
and that's really important. Glenn is good on defense too, but
he's not that smart."

A few moments later, we sat down at the dinner table.
Mr. Nixon raised a toast to the birthday girl. "You're still my
great, big, beautiful birthday girl." Everyone at the table cried.

Mr. Nixon sipped his glass of wine. He complimented it enthusiastically, beaming toward his hosts, the Drowns.

After the dinner, there was much talk about the 1976 campaign. Someone, maybe Ben Stein, asked why Goldwater was slow in coming out in support of Ford. Nixon leaned into the question enthusiastically: "Why? Because he's a goddamn drunken asshole. He's been having drinking problems for years. Now he's just out of control. He was for a while. He never even tried to win in 1964."

Somehow, the subject of Mr. Nixon's brother, Donald, came up. He had recently been mocked in the media. "He's not a bad fellow. He's not like Lyndon Johnson's brother, Sam. They kept him up on the third floor of the White House for years."

Mr. Nixon shared an anecdote he had been told by H. L. Hunt, the oil mogul. An oil driller had a brother who was always whining for a job. So the driller gave him a job on a dynamite truck. The truck blew up.

No one laughed.

Talk turned to RN's language on the White House tapes. "Some people thought mine was bad. They should've heard LBJ's language. He was amazing," recounted Mr. Nixon, who told the story with a hearty laugh. We all laughed too.

"Why aren't more people supporting Reagan?" Mr. Nixon asked. Mr. Nixon did not say who he liked, but he did say that more people would support Reagan if he got on TV more.

Then he got on the subject of Professor Zbigniew Brzezinski, a huge star in foreign policy. He had been my teacher at Columbia long before and was now advising the nation at large and especially Jimmy Carter, then a candidate.

I told Mr. Nixon that I found Professor Brzezinski to be a fine teacher, although I did recall his saying that there was no possible way that North Vietnam could ever defeat the south.

Mr. Nixon said he had asked Henry Kissinger about Brzezinski. Imitating Kissinger's famous accent, Mr. Nixon said that Kissinger had said, "He is nothing but an opportunist." Mr. Nixon laughed lightly and asked, "Can you imagine that? Henry saying that about someone else?" We all laughed, but carefully, because we knew RN loved Kissinger in his heart of hearts.

Helen Drown talked about a local election in or near Rancho Palos Verdes. A Black Republican was running. Ms. Drown said, "Jews will never support a Republican."

An odd comment, I thought, considering who was in the room.

RN looked at me and asked, "Why don't the Jews like me? If it weren't for me, there wouldn't be an Israel. You may not know it, but Golda Meir knows it."

"Sir, I assure you, I know it." I told the room about my experience with the Israeli students who were visiting the White House the day Nixon left the White House. As I told him, the Israeli schoolchildren were terrified, and many of them were in tears about the prospect of a world without RN as president of the United States and protector of Israel. "They know who saved them, and they love you through and through."

RN nodded in agreement and looked genuinely moved. To me, he often looked genuinely moved.

Talk then turned to other matters, such as how Mr. Nixon and his son-in-law David would play golf the following day.

At the end of the night, Mr. Nixon got into the back of his car. Julie leaned in to hug him, and he hugged her back.

"You're still my great, big, beautiful baby girl," he said to her and hugged her again, and then his car drove off. Julie, who is the thinnest of the thin, had tears in her eyes. So did we all.

It was a memorable birthday party.

CHAPTER TWELVE

IN CHARGE OF FREEDOM ITSELF

My first visit to RN, more than a year before Julie's birthday party, coincided roughly with the Fall of Saigon in April 1975. That was when I was still working at the *Wall Street Journal*. I was staying at the fabulous Beverly Hills Hotel. I was leasing a Mercedes-Benz 450SL convertible, all courtesy of the Dow Jones. And there I was racing down the San Diego Freeway on a brilliantly sunny day. My ex-wife, with whom I was in the process of reconciling, was next to me and loving the experience.

We were waved through the Marine guard gates at San Clemente. We parked in a small lot and then were led to Mr. Nixon's office. Mr. Nixon made a comment about how beautiful my ex-wife was (and is) and then said (and bear in mind, these are *not* exact transcriptions), "Can you believe how those idiots in Congress threw away Vietnam? Can you believe we had a deal worked out that was going to save South Vietnam? Henry and Bill Rogers and I had it worked out, and it was going well."

"Yes, Mr. President," I said.

"It was a simple deal. We recognized perfectly well that the Communists were going to beat the south if it were just a case of man-to-man fighting. They were far better disciplined. They had party commissars and political police right behind the Vietcong and the North Vietnamese Army. These were tough guys. They were ready to shoot anyone, officers and soldiers, in the back who did not advance when the commissars told them to advance.

"We had total air superiority. We would strafe them and even hit them with napalm, but they would keep on coming. When this war is over—and it will someday be over—and an official death count comes out, historians will be stunned at the tally of deaths of the Communists. But meanwhile, they just kept coming. So we made a deal with them. They had to stop advancing southward a certain amount north of Saigon. If they didn't, we would bomb Haiphong Harbor, just like we did in Operation Rolling Thunder, which was what got them to stop a couple of years ago."

"Right," I said.

"So then I get thrown out, for what, no one exactly knows, although the *Washington Post* says they know. And that jerk Walter Cronkite says he knows. But they don't know what I did wrong, and I don't know because the media was out to get me. They have been since the Hiss case. I literally do not know what I was supposed to have done."

"Of course."

"The truth is that I didn't do anything wrong except to help my friends and the people who worked for me. I didn't do anything even remotely wrong by historic standards. But when the media powers are out to get you, they'll take anything and wrap it around your neck. They'll take a broken shoelace and wrap it around your neck and hang you with it."

"You've always been loyal," I said to him.

"Yes. Too loyal. That was what did it. Meanwhile, Jerry Ford took over as president. He did a great job. But the media was out to get him too. They actually tried to make Jerry Ford, the best athlete that was ever in the White House, look clumsy.

"Then the Democratic Congress stepped in and reneged on America's deal with the Communists. They said they would not do anything if the Communists came down Highway 1 all the way to Saigon. That was the complete betrayal of an ally we had pledged to support. That was a disaster in terms of international relations."

He patted King Timahoe's head, a gesture, I soon learned, he often made when he wished to emphasize some point or another.

"People think that the Army of Vietnam was completely incompetent and cowardly. Not true. There were units of the Army of Vietnam fighting on the steps to the capitol in Saigon. They were fighting and dying for what they had wanted all along: a Vietnam at least somewhat in the image of the United States, with a government elected by the people.

"They didn't betray us. We betrayed them. If we had kept our word and bombed the hell out of Haiphong Harbor—not a civilian target, by the way—and strafed the Communists as they approached Saigon, it might have made a major difference."

I asked him, "Mr. President, how big a difference would it have made?"

Mr. Nixon looked pained. "We have to go back into history. Could we have won that war? I don't know. I know that the south was largely Catholic. They did not want to be ruled by Communists. They had seen millions of killings, real slave labor camps run by the Communists. There was a steady stream of anti-Communists going south after the armistice. And they knew they were going to have to fight and likely die to keep their country free. But they came anyway.

"Could they have fought long enough and hard enough to defeat the Communists? It happened in Korea. Or at least it happened enough for there to be a long-lasting armistice. And we helped the South Koreans a great deal. And by the way, look at South Korea. It's become one of the major industrial powers on earth. And they were in ruins in 1953. They're an amazing people.

"Could the South Vietnamese have held their own against the Communists?

"We don't know. We do know we betrayed our friends. It looks bad. And it is bad. What many so-called experts don't follow is that there is a moral dimension to politics, domestic or foreign." (Here he made a mocking look with his eyes, as if to say that he did not recognize the concept of "experts" in foreign policy or anywhere else.)

"It's not just that dots are moved around and colors get changed on a map. People get murdered. People get sent to slave labor camps. Children are taken away from their parents and sent to live with loyal party members. In Cambodia, which the Communists have pretty much entirely taken over by now, the Communists make the children murder their own parents. They bury the parents up to their necks, and then the kids are ordered to take stout sticks, like axe handles, and beat their parents to death.

"It's hard to believe that anything so horrible could actually happen, but it's happening. And we let the Cambodians in for it.

We told them that if they fought against the Communists, the Khmer Rouge, as they called themselves, we would be on their side. And then we ran for cover.

"How many Democrats or so-called Republicans realized that their votes and their words against me would result in children being forced at gunpoint to beat their parents' brains out? What could I possibly have done that would merit such hatred in the hearts of the congressional powers? And the media powers? They tell themselves and they tell the world how brave they are to stand up to Nixon.

"That wasn't brave. I wasn't going to do anything to hurt them. They knew it well. I was already getting beaten by them, and no one lifted a finger against the media. Far from it. They were invited to ever more luxurious parties at Mrs. Graham's house on R Street. As I was being shown the door, the Communists were creating ever more atrocities. There was a one-to-one connection. The Vietcong and the North Vietnamese knew that once I was gone, they could do anything and get away with it.

"I'll say it again—I just wonder how many of the editorial writers and TV commentators knew that pushing me out here to San Clemente would mean even more deaths of the innocent. I wonder how many even considered it at all."

I sat stunned and amazed. Why hadn't Nixon talked like this a couple of months or years ago? This was the most lucid explanation of why Nixon should have stayed in office that I had ever heard.

"Meanwhile, we at home doubt ourselves," Mr. Nixon said. "And we should. We did a terrible betrayal. Look, Benjy, we're at war with a genuinely evil force. Communism."

Then he paused for a moment in a gesture that I came to learn was habitual. He stared me in the face and asked, "You agree with that, Ben?"

"I agree, sir. But if the war goes on, people get killed too. When I was younger, I asked my father-in-law, the father of this beautiful woman here who is my wife, a man who had graduated from West Point on D-day, June 6, 1944, and who had been awarded the Silver Star for combat gallantry in Germany, then had served for a year of combat in Vietnam and gotten the Bronze Star and the Distinguished Service Medal in Vietnam, what he thought about our marching against the war in Vietnam."

"The Silver Star? That's a big one. The Distinguished Service Medal? That's a big one too." He looked at my wife. "I hope you appreciated him. Did you?"

"I did once Benjy taught me to appreciate him," my wife said. "Before that, not anywhere near as much as I could have."

Nixon nodded. "Good point. How many of us appreciate our parents as much as they deserve? Not many. You agree with that, Benjy?" Mr. Nixon asked with a smile, the smile recognizing that he found it amusing that my wife referred to me as Benjy.

"What did he say? What did your father say about your demonstrating about the war in Vietnam?"

"He said to demonstrate against it any time possible," my wife said. "He said it was a 'meat grinder' that we couldn't possibly win and that we should do anything possible to give up and come home."

Mr. Nixon looked thoughtful. "And he was right. The whole reason that America is America is that we have freedom of speech and of assembly. But how does it look to our allies around the world if we lose a war against a third-world country like Vietnam? What rank was your father-in-law?"

"Full colonel," I said.

"And he was in serious combat? That's impressive. That's a brave man."

"You bet, Mr. President," I agreed. "A superstar."

"But he was in charge of a few hundred men, or maybe a thousand men. I'm in charge of the whole country and, in a way, in charge of freedom itself. That's a whole different story, and in many ways, a very sad story.

"You know, Ben, your father used to say that there were some problems to which there are simply no easy answers. And I think he might have added that there are some problems that just don't have any answers at all."

Then he added, "You agree with that? Even at your age?"

"I do indeed, sir. Why was man put on earth to die? That's one of them," I said.

"A deep thinker," said Mr. Nixon. "Like your father, a deep thinker. You are extremely lucky to have had such a smart man as your father. And a very successful man. Very few people get that kind of advantage in life. A successful father is a big leg up in life."

"You are very kind," I said. "Believe me, sir, I am very grateful."

"And loyal. Your father. Never a second's doubt that he was loyal. And a great sense of humor. Remember a few years ago when he had that stroke? An ambulance came and took him out to the Washington Hospital Center. I called him there the same day, and he told me he had lost vision in one of his eyes. I told him how sorry I was. You know what he said, Ben?"

"Yes, I do, sir. He said that half of what he was supposed to read wasn't worth reading anyway."

"Exactly," said Mr. Nixon. "Exactly.

"Meanwhile, let's look at the world. There are two great forces. Dictatorial, murderous Communism, which leads to millions—tens of millions—starving to death, tens of millions more being murdered by the state. And on the other side, freedom. It leads to prosperity and plenty and individual rights and dignity.

"Just in the time I've been in government service, the Communists, the killers, the ones who make millions starve to death, have taken over China, North Korea, most of Indochina, and the mass murders in Asia have been breathtaking.

"I like to think that the best things I ever did were save Israel, keep the Soviets from taking over the whole Middle East, visit China and offer a glimpse of what a free enterprise system could do, and maybe slow down the march of a cruel variant of Communism in China.

"The best thing General Eisenhower did was to convince the Soviets that we really would use the nuclear bomb if Russia invaded Germany and France. And he saved Europe from Soviet control. That was a truly enormous achievement.

"You know, I can remember very well when the columnists and commentators used to portray General Eisenhower as if he were a dopey farm boy who happened to become president by a stroke of luck or fate. Herblock used to make cartoons of him in the *Washington Post* that made him out to be a moron, pushed around by Joe McCarthy.

"Nothing could be further from the truth. Ike was smart enough to supervise the greatest amphibious invasion of all time, the D-day landings in Normandy. Then he supervised the Western allies as they fought their way into Germany. Ike also fully orchestrated the congressional weakening and virtual decapitation of McCarthy. I was his chief go-to guy in that effort. It wasn't easy either. Oh, no," he added, shaking his head from side to side so that his cheeks wavered like waves coming into a shoreline. "McCarthy did not have many friends in the newspapers, but he had plenty of friends in the Senate."

"The European theater," I chimed in. "That's where my father-in-law did the combat gallantry that got him the Silver Star. Outside a town called Zeitlin. He was in a fierce firefight with the SS on the day Hitler committed suicide. He told me that the Germans are ferocious fighters."

"You bet," Mr. Nixon said. "They're an amazing people when well led and dreadful when poorly led. Eisenhower was of partly German ancestry, by the way. At least I think so.

"And now in Vietnam, we see another case of vicious dictatorial Communism beating the West," Mr. Nixon said, returning to his line of discussion. "How does this look to the world?"

"It looks bad," I said.

"More than bad," he said. "And why do the Democrats in Congress help the Communists in Vietnam win?"

"I don't mean to argue with you," I answered, "but I guess they thought the war was unwinnable and so we might as well get out."

"Right," said RN. "And maybe they were right. I don't assume that all Democrats are always wrong. 'Scoop' Jackson was as great a senator as there has been in my lifetime. Hubert Humphrey was a great man. But I have an image of a Vietnamese man who fought alongside the U.S. Army in Vietnam being snatched up from his house after the Communists won and taken to a slave labor camp or being shot or, if he were in Cambodia, getting murdered by his kids on the orders of the Khmer Rouge.

"And a helluva lot of blame attaches to us. So how can we be proud of ourselves and believe we will always win because we are morally right?"

At that point, without much ado, Mr. Nixon laboriously got up from his seat and walked around the room for a moment.

"I have to rest for a while now," he said, and he pressed a button on his desk. His assistant came in. "My legs have never been the same since my embolism. I have to get a bit of exercise. I didn't know this talk would last so long." And here he reached out and shook my hand and then kissed my wife on the cheek. "Deep thinker," he said again, touching his right index finger to his right temple. "Deep thinker. Just like his dad. How is your dad? I recall he had some heart troubles. How is Mildred?"

And here my brains blew right out of my head. I will tell you why, if I may. When my mother was a little girl in the small, mountainous Upstate New York town of Monticello, which had many Jews who had lung problems, she and her father would go on certain days to the homes of Jews in the area to ask for contributions to the Jewish National Fund or whatever it was called then and solicit contributions for Eretz Yisrael, which in Hebrew means "homeland Israel." At that time, in the 1920s, for Jews to have their own country was a dream. Now Israel is a small but superpotent state. It owes its existence in very large measure to the heroism and love of President Richard M. Nixon. And now I was sitting in the office of Richard

Nixon, and he was calling my mother by her first name. My little, diminutive mother, five feet one in her stocking feet, by her first name. My mother, still very much alive at that point, would have been in seventh heaven. It was dizzying.

I thanked RN profusely. "My pop is fine, and my mother sends her love and admiration to you every instant." Mr. Nixon nodded and shook our hands. Then I walked out with my wife. "Come back any time," he said to Alex. "I don't get many deep thinkers in here. Bring Benjy."

Alex and I drove back to LA along the 405. I was basically in a trance. Alex, who had never been anywhere near as hearty a fan of Nixon as I was, had been converted. She was Saul on the way to Tarsus. By that point, she would have done anything for RN.

CHAPTER THIRTEEN

A SHONDA—A DISGRACE

I did not wait long to take Mr. Nixon up on his invitation. I was soon on my way back there in my "new" car, a slightly used gray Mercedes 450SLC. It was a dream come true.

This time, I did not have my wife with me. She was back in DC working at her corporate law firm, Donovan, Leisure, Newton & Irvine. I drove down in breathtaking time. This was in late '76.

I was shown into Mr. Nixon's office, which seemed to me to have even more U.S. military and naval flags on poles than before. His beautiful secretary, Diane Sawyer, later to become a superfamous TV persona, was there. She greeted me cheerfully and then left the room.

"There are a couple of things I wanted to pursue," Mr. Nixon said. He was—for the first time I had ever seen him—not wearing a sports jacket or a blazer. Instead, he was wearing a dark-blue windbreaker with a presidential seal over the right breast pocket.

"I think I mentioned how 'the world' would have reacted if Israel had used nuclear weapons in the Yom Kippur War and how our own foreign and domestic policies always had to be

catered in a way to take a bow to the opinion of 'the world.'
I used to think that way too." When he said "the world," he
held up air quotes with his hands to signify how imaginary the
concept was.

(Actually, I did not recall RN dwelling on that issue.)

"When I was a senator," Mr. Nixon continued, "when I was
Ike's VP, when I was president, we always discussed policy initiatives or continuations from many perspectives. One of them
was how the world would react to events and words coming
from us."

"I am sure," I said.

"But that was all nonsense. It's just like trying to weigh
smoke. More to the point, it's like trying to herd cats—only
cats with sharp claws and no weight. The world is a fiction. It
exists, all right. It's on the map. But it doesn't do anything. At
least not anything useful.

"I often have visitors from Israel who still like me."

"I know it well, Mr. President," I said. "The afternoon of the
day you resigned, I had the task, assigned on a rotating basis,
but probably because I am Jewish, of speaking to a group of
about thirty visiting Israeli high school students. They were
in tears. Literally in tears of fear about what would happen to
Israel without Nixon there to protect them."

Mr. Nixon looked genuinely gratified. I continued, "I can
vividly recall a beautiful young Israeli woman crying and asking, 'Who else in the whole world will love Israel the way
Mr. Nixon has?'"

"They were right to be worried," Mr. Nixon said. "The world
is just a fantasy. It's something like an imaginary jury pool of
totally upright citizens of a community who will condemn

morally bad nations or leaders and uphold and protect the innocent.

"I occasionally get visits from Jewish survivors of Nazi death camps. They tell me that when they first got swept up by the Gestapo and sent to the camps, they would think, 'The world must know about this. If the world knew, they would put a stop to the genocide.' But soon they realized that there was no 'world' that was watching over them. There were nations that had their own problems. There were individuals and groups that were interested in the genocide but did not want to risk their own intelligence services or cryptographers, like the British. There were nations and peoples who just did not like the Jews to start with.

"The world is no friend to the Jews and never has been. The world, with one exception, did nothing to stop African slavery when it was going full blast in the eighteenth and nineteenth centuries. There is still slavery in Africa and Asia. There was immense slavery and mass murder in the Soviet Union before Hitler came to power in Germany. The world did nothing about it. The world in the person of the most famous columnists and 'reporters' [air quotes again] actually praised Stalin as he was sending millions to their deaths. 'You can't make an omelet without breaking eggs' was how the media said it as Stalin starved millions of Ukrainians to death.

"There is still slavery and mass murder in certain parts of the Communist entity. The world does nothing about it. When we had slavery and the most hideous kinds of abuses of Black men and women in this great country, the world did very little to stop it."

"Although the British did ban slavery or the use of slave ships in the first half of the nineteenth century," I interrupted.

Mr. Nixon smiled. "The deep thinker at work," he said. "The point is that the world was not what stepped in to stop the Hitler genocide against the Jews. It was the combatants—the Western Allies and Soviet Russia—that stopped the Nazi genocide by beating the hell out of the Nazis.

"And even at that, the Reds were running their own mass-murder camps while the Nazis were beaten, and afterward . . ." Mr. Nixon paused and stared at me. "Stalin probably killed more Soviets than Hitler even when the Wehrmacht was on Russian soil. Did you know that?"

"I am afraid you'll find it hard to believe, but I did know that," I said. "My mother was a ferocious anti-Communist all her life. She kept me well informed."

"Ah, Mildred," Mr. Nixon said. "The real deep thinker in the Stein family."

He said it with a smile. He liked that theme. And, again, I loved the truth that Mr. Nixon, my hero, Israel's hero, called my mother by her first name. He did it a lot, and I always loved it.

"And now the world watches the Khmer Rouge atrocities in Cambodia and does nothing," Mr. Nixon went on. "But I read that the Khmer Rouge is nipping at the heels of the North Vietnamese over a border issue. The North Vietnamese will not put up with that, I suspect. They're tough. They're not the world, but they're tough, and as we have learned, they are well armed and don't like to be pushed around."

(Within a short time, the Communists in Vietnam proved Mr. Nixon right. They invaded Cambodia, or Kampuchea, as it came to be called, and kicked out the Khmer Rouge. The "leadership" of the Khmer Rouge fled into the jungle. Pol Pot, heir to one of the most prosperous families in Cambodia as a young man, leader of by far the most brutal repression in South Asia ever, was captured and died in captivity in 1979, or so it is said. Interestingly enough, the only government in the area that supported Pol Pot's genocidal maniacs was Communist China, which had been befriended by Mr. Nixon while Pol Pot was still alive.)

(I later told the story about the Israeli students the day RN resigned at Julie Nixon Eisenhower's birthday party in 1976, which I have already discussed, and RN was polite enough not to remind me I had already told him the tale.)

"At any event," Mr. Nixon said, "if the world expects that the North Vietnamese will be dramatically more humane to the Vietnamese people because of the world's expectations, I am afraid they are expecting quite a lot."

There was more small talk, probably about dogs, before we launched into phase two of Mr. Nixon's thoughts about "the world."

He had actually leaned back in his chair and closed his eyes to rest before he started up again.

"'The world' is made up of a lot of different countries and different peoples. Some of them have consciences and some don't. And only when it suits the leaders does the conscience of 'the world' come into play.

"Tell me, Benjy, when was the last time you saw the conscience of the world come into play in a huge way?"

"Mr. President, that was when you saved Israel, at life-or-death risk to the United States."

In a few seconds' time, Mr. Nixon looked proud, agonized, and then unpleasantly amused. I said to him, "I know,

Mr. President. I know. It was a deep and horrible tragedy for America's Jews to have failed you when you needed them so desperately."

There was a full minute's silence, and then Mr. Nixon shook his head. He said, "Human nature. It's human nature."

"Yes, but no national leader has ever been as good to us Jews as you have been, and none has ever been so mistreated as you have been. And that was not the world reaching out to save Israel. It was you, Mr. President. And when you did, the people in Muncie were just as unconcerned as the people in Buenos Aires. And the Jews of America were largely unconcerned as well."

Mr. Nixon paused for a good long time and then spoke. "Why?" Mr. Nixon asked. "Why?"

"I don't know. I just don't know. It's a disgrace. It's what we Jews called *a Shonda*. That means a disgrace. Just a disgrace."

There was a lull of a few minutes, and then Mr. Nixon said, "Your parents were always grateful. I can remember very well when the Russian antiaircraft missiles were shooting down the IDF jets right and left. And some extremely important Jews in the administration would not stand up for Israel. Some very important ones, but I remember your father did something extremely out of character for him. He asked for and got an appointment with me. Literally as the war was raging. And he asked me—no, he begged me—to help Israel. Somehow he knew we had black boxes that could jam those Russian missiles. And he and Len Garment just implored me to help Israel, with his face flushed and his eyes moist.

"I won't say for a minute that's what changed my mind. But what I will say is that I was moved and impressed that a man as careful and sober and patriotic as Herb Stein made such an emotional plea."

"God bless you," I said.

At that point, an assistant came in to see Mr. Nixon and brought him a plate of cottage cheese and catsup and offered me a cheeseburger with catsup and salt and a Diet Pepsi.

"We're not going to let Israel go under, Ben," Mr. Nixon said. "We're not going to let Russia push us around all over the world."

"God bless you," I said again.

"People say I'm anti-Semitic," Mr. Nixon said. "That's the biggest lie about me in a lifetime of lies about me."

"The Israelis still love you," I said.

"And they should. But why do the Israeli Jews love Nixon and the American Jews don't ever stop hating me?"

"Not all of them," I said, "but way too many. I don't know why. It just became the fashion at some point among America's Jews, and it just never went away. It had something to do with a completely mistaken belief that Republicans were anti-Semites, starting from when the Jews came over to Ellis Island."

"But the Democrats were the real anti-Semites," Mr. Nixon said with relish. "If you look at the wild anti-Semites of the 1920s, like 'Pitchfork Ben' Tillman of South Carolina, they were all Democrats. People think FDR was a great pal of the Jews, but that was not so. He stood up for the Jews from time to time, but mostly, he said, 'Hands off.' And even when we were in the war, he could have bombed the rail lines going into Auschwitz. He could have done it, but he never did. Can you imagine if I did that? Or didn't do it?"

I did not know how to respond, so I remained silent for a few seconds and then said, "Mr. President, the misconceptions about you are literally limitless. The Jews have held some of the worst of them. I'll say it again: American Jews just have the basic misconception that the Republicans and you in particular are anti-Semites. I agree that it's a disgrace considering how good you have been to Israel and to American Jews—like my father, in particular."

"I didn't do myself any favors in the Jewish world with my own words in the transcripts too," he said. "Those were ill-chosen words indeed. I make a lot of mistakes." He paused and then smiled and waved around the room as if to say, "Note this world as opposed to the Oval Office." He smiled ruefully and added, "I guess that's obvious."

Then he closed his eyes and said, "Now, I really am tired and have to rest. We'll talk again soon."

CHAPTER FOURTEEN

THE MOST CAPABLE PEOPLE ON EARTH

My next meeting with RN came shortly after a blowup in the Middle East. In it, as usual, the Palestinians had showered rockets on civilian targets in Israel. Israel would follow up with air attacks on Hamas or other Palestinian targets.

The mass media would show bombed-out hospitals and wounded or dead Palestinian children but never, or rarely, the Israeli civilian casualties. Nixon started out the session with his usual anger toward the media: "And so many of these media people are Jewish!" he said. "They really gave up thinking they had any allegiance to either Israel or the truth a long time ago. How did you get to where you are about telling the truth and sticking up for Israel? You're in the media too."

"My parents worshiped America, and they loved Israel too," I said. "That was an article of faith in our home."

Mr. Nixon loved lists, and what I had said was enough to start him on one.

"Who do you see as the most capable people on earth?" he asked me, somewhat out of the blue.

"Well, you and Julie first," I said with a smile.

Mr. Nixon laughed lightly. "No. I mean as a people," he said.

"Sir, I have never tried to figure it out."

"To me, it comes out pretty clearly. First, the Israeli Jews. What they have done with that stretch of donkey trails and rocks and desert is beyond belief. For them to have won the Arab-Israeli War in 1948 when no one would help them; when the British were tossing in with the Jordanians; when no country would sell them arms, including the United States; when they were outnumbered one hundred to one by the Arab armies, that was incredible. No one thought they could even hold their own. Instead, they expanded their borders and made the country contiguous instead of a small group of outposts."

"Yes," I agreed. "Amazing."

"Then for the Israelis to hold back the Syrians and the Egyptians and the Iraqis and the Jordanians and everyone else when the Arabs were getting up-to-date weapons from the Soviets and while we still had an arms embargo against Israel—that would have seemed impossible. But for Israel to have just kicked the Egyptians, armed to the teeth with Russian gear, out of Sinai and to have seized the Suez Canal, that was just impossible to believe had even happened.

"And we made a mistake bullying Israel in the UN over it. But it was just right out of science fiction," RN added. "Although to be fair, I don't recall ever reading any science fiction in my life."

"The whole story of Israel is science fiction and Bible fiction at the same time," I replied. "And you are the Moses—more than the Moses—of the story. Moses did not risk his own country to save the Jews. You did."

Mr. Nixon laughed and brushed off the compliment with a wave of his hand. Then he continued, "But the American Jews still never liked me."

"Some did," I said with a smile. "Some still do."

"Ah, Herb and Mildred," he said. "And Benjy."

There was a moment of silence, and then Mr. Nixon said, "And then to have won the Yom Kippur War and finally made real, defensible borders against full-scale Soviet help."

"That was your doing, Mr. President."

Mr. Nixon waved away my praise again. "It had to be done. Or the Soviets would have controlled the whole Middle East and a helluva lot of oil. Meanwhile, because of a few trivial remarks I made, some people think I'm an anti-Semite."

"Some people think Hitler is alive and well and in Argentina," I said.

Mr. Nixon laughed. "And now Israel has by far the most powerful armed force in the Middle East and is one of the leading scientific powers on earth. The average Israeli will soon have a standard of living higher than the average Englishman. That would have been considered unimaginable in 1948. And this with just the few ragged people who managed to escape Hitler's death camps and the Jews from all over the world who wanted a better life. The same story as the United States.

"And Israel started out with a U.S. president, Harry Truman, whose wife, Bess, made him swear he would never allow Jews in their living room when they lived back in Missouri. And now Jews are a power in the United States. Not because of American Jews but because we respect a nation that can fight so well for itself.

"You're pals with Peter Flanigan, right?"

"Yes, indeed," I said. "I'm his biggest fan."

"Peter used to say that it didn't take the most up-to-date weapons to win wars or deter wars. It took guts. And Israel has guts."

"So wonderfully true," I agreed.

"So after the Israeli Jews, among the world's peoples, the most able are the Japanese. Small country. No natural resources to speak of. But they came close to controlling the whole Pacific and a large part of the world.

"And cruel, as we saw in Nanjing. Would never surrender. Even the Germans said the Japanese were too cruel and admired how tough they were. The Germans would surrender eventually if they were surrounded. But the Japanese would fight until the last man was dead. Now they have a manufacturing power only second to us, and we are a much bigger country with many mineral resources and an agriculture sector that's the most successful on earth."

(I note here that this was said by Mr. Nixon at the time Japan Inc. seemed unstoppably poised to take over the world. Obviously, that has changed. China has taken on the mantle Japan used to wear.)

Mr. Nixon resumed: "Then the British, who used to control about one-third of the earth. They were a nation the size of Alabama with a very small population. By their brains, especially the Scots, they whipped themselves into extraordinary self-discipline and, with that, basically conquered the world. And the Irish, who are an astonishingly smart, brave people. I'm partly Irish, in case you didn't know."

"I know," I said. "Peter Flanigan told me."

Mr. Nixon smiled. "The Steins, along with the Nixons, are part of the Peter Flanigan fan club." Mr. Nixon paused and then said, "And then the Germans, again with a small country by world standards—by extreme aggressiveness and self-discipline, they were close twice in this century to subduing all of

Europe. Cruel as cruel can be, but tough. And then the French, who did prodigies under Napoleon. And just to make it clear, then the Irish, and they were the best fighters in the British Armed Forces. And then the Americans, who became the biggest power on earth.

"That was largely because of the kind of people we had here: large numbers of Germans, large numbers of British and Irish, and large numbers of French and Italians. And, of course, the Jews. The Jews are the smartest people on earth. And the American Jews are successful.

"But they can't even be compared with the Israeli Jews. The American Jews are smart and resourceful. But they can't be compared with the Israeli Jews, who accomplished so much with so little. God bless them."

"And then?" I asked. "And then?"

"The Chinese. They've been poorly led for a very long time. They were splintered for a very long time. Now that they're unified, eventually, there will be no stopping them. But that will take a long time. And who's to say they won't be splintered again?"

"The Arabs?" I asked. "The sub-Saharan Africans? The South Americans? The American Blacks?"

Mr. Nixon waved the questions aside. "It's early still. They're not anywhere great right now. But they can learn. They can make themselves global players, but they haven't yet."

"The Russians?"

"Obviously an amazingly brave, smart people. If they hadn't been so tough, Hitler would have won the war. So we owe a lot to the Russians. It is a shame that we and the Russians are not friends. That's because of really sick, dangerous Communists, especially Stalin. Still, we should be friends with the Russians, if not the Communists. Most Americans do not even come close to realizing how important the Russians were to saving the world. As brave as a people can be. And smart. The best weapon makers on earth. But not really a first-world power yet. If they can get out from under the yoke of Communism, they can do anything.

"But when a people have been enslaved so long, lived in terror so long, there's really no way to tell how long until they recover."

At that point, Mr. Nixon announced that he was tired and wanted to rest. I thanked him for his time and his wisdom. "You're the deep thinker here," he said. "Benjy, you'll go far."

Then I walked out the door to my fabulous car and was gone.

CHAPTER FIFTEEN

AN ORDINARY MAN WEARING A NIXON MASK

The second-to-last time I saw Mr. Nixon in San Clemente, Julie and David had moved to a home on Capistrano Beach. They invited my wife and me to meet their baby. Moments after we got there and were admiring their baby, Mr. and Mrs. Nixon appeared at the door.

He was in a gray suit. He looked to me like an ordinary man wearing a Nixon mask. He played with the baby for some time, and then he left.

I do not recall a word he said.

*   *   *

The last time I saw Mr. Nixon in San Clemente was just before he and Mrs. Nixon moved to New Jersey. His local friends, of whom he had many, had arranged a going-away party for him and Pat. There were about a hundred of us ranging from child-hood friends to friends from the very last days in the White House, like my wife and me.

We were all gathered around the pool, eating hors d'oeuvres and looking at the sea. La Casa Pacifica was a truly spectacular home with Spanish revival architecture with large lawns and a small golf course overlooking the Pacific. It would be hard for Mr. Nixon to give up this home, I thought. Not to mention his friends of a lifetime.

Mr. Nixon walked around and greeted us all by name, and then I noticed that he disappeared. Nowhere to be seen.

I walked over to the residence. There, through an immense floor-to-ceiling window, was Mr. Nixon, sitting in a deep-red easy chair, with a tray at his right arm loaded with cottage cheese and catsup, and watching a baseball game on TV. The sound of a crowd cheering for the home team roared from the TV, and there sat the peacemaker in front of the TV.

Alone.

*   *   *

Richard Nixon died on April 22, 1994. My pal Larry Dietz called me at Morton's on Melrose to tell me the grim news. The next day or maybe the day after that, he lay in state in the Richard Nixon Library and Museum in Yorba Linda. I drove out there and parked a mile or two away. I then joined the largest crowd I had ever seen in person. Hundreds of thousands of fans of the peacemaker walked slowly down the eight lanes of Yorba Linda Boulevard in total silence, then passed by the coffin of Richard M. Nixon of Yorba Linda. Many of the mourners were in tears. Some knelt and crossed themselves as they honored him.

The next day, the *Los Angeles Times* did not even mention it.

EPILOGUE

The greatest honor history can bestow
is the title of peacemaker.
—President Nixon's epitaph

Nixon, the greatest peacemaker of all time, who gave us a "generation of peace," was humiliated over trivial matters that were way below what other presidents have done—kicked out, name blackened.

But we who were there know the truth. In kicking out Richard Nixon, we kicked out a great man and a peacemaker.

It was almost fifty years ago that we as a nation kicked out of office the greatest foreign policy maestro we have ever had—Richard M. Nixon, working closely with a genuine genius, Henry Kissinger. Richard Nixon, the peacemaker with the Quaker mother, made up with Mao and Chou Enlai, although China's streets still ran red with the blood of the Cultural Revolution.

By so doing, he, in a general way, encircled the Soviets and made certain they knew they were on the losing side of the Cold War.

Nixon made peace possible in the Middle East by assuring Israel that it could not be defeated, despite an amazing showing by the Egyptian Army in the Yom Kippur War.

Nixon ended the war in Vietnam and brought home the prisoners.

Nixon signed the first major strategic arms limitation treaty with the Soviets. It involved real cuts, done out of mutual respect and fear.

Mr. Nixon said he would leave us a "generation of peace," and he did. Who among us would not wish him to be back to guide us right now? I miss him every day.

I worked for a peacemaker. Blessed are they, and I will never turn my back on Richard Nixon. If I have nothing else to remember me by, this is all I want: I was the servant and the friend of a peacemaker.

Your Humble Servant,
Ben Stein

INDEX

ABOUT THE AUTHOR

BEN STEIN is a writer, actor, economist, and lawyer. He writes the "Dreemz" column for Newsmax and "Ben Stein's Diary" for the *American Spectator* and is the host of *The World According to Ben Stein* podcast. His comedic role as the droning economics teacher in *Ferris Bueller's Day Off* is by far the most widely viewed scene of economics teaching in history and has been ranked as one of the fifty most famous scenes in movie history. But in real life, Ben Stein is a *New York Times* bestselling author and a powerful thinker on economics, politics, education, history, and motivation—and like his father, Herbert Stein, Ben is considered one of the great humorists on political economy and how life works in this nation.

Stein has a bachelor's degree with honors in economics from Columbia and studied economics at the graduate level at Yale. He is a graduate of Yale Law School (valedictorian of his class by the election of his classmates in 1970) and has as diverse a résumé as any person in America. That résumé includes a poverty lawyer for poor people in New Haven, a trade regulation lawyer for the FTC, a speechwriter for presidents Nixon and Ford, a columnist and editorial writer for the *Wall Street Journal* and the *New York Times*, and a teacher of law and economics at University of California Santa Cruz (undergrads) and Pepperdine University (law school and undergrads). Along with his many movie, TV, and commercials roles that have made him the most famous economics teacher in the world, Stein was the cohost, along with his friend Jimmy Kimmel, of the pathbreaking Comedy Central game show *Win Ben Stein's Money*, which won seven Emmys, including ones for Ben and Jimmy for best game show hosts, making Ben the only well-known economist to win an Emmy.

Stein is the *New York Times* bestselling author or coauthor of over thirty books of nonfiction and fiction, including *The World According to Ben Stein* and *The Capitalist Code*, and he has written extensively for both film and TV and is a regular commentator on TV and radio, including Newsmax, Fox News, *CBS News Sunday Morning*, CNN, and more.

Ben is blessed to live in Los Angeles with his wife of fifty-five years, Alexandra, and various cats and dogs, and he is a proud father and grandfather.

Visit Ben Stein:
www.mrbenstein.com